THE NIGHT
MY MOTHER
MET
BRUCE LEE

Paisley Rekdal

 Pantheon Books, New York

THE NIGHT
MY MOTHER
MET
BRUCE LEE

Observations on Not Fitting In

All rights reserved under International and Pan-American Copyright
Conventions. Published in the United States by Pantheon Books,
a division of Random House, Inc., New York, and simultaneously
in Canada by Random House of Canada Limited, Toronto.

Pantheon Books and colophon are registered trademarks of Random
House, Inc.

The essay "We Do Not Live Here, We Are Only Visitors" was
originally published in slightly different form in *Grand Tour*
magazine in 1995.

All the events in this account are factual, but the time frame in
which they occurred and the names and identifying characteristics
of certain individuals have been changed in order to afford them a
measure of privacy.

Library of Congress Cataloging-in-Publication Data

Rekdal, Paisley.
    The night my mother met Bruce Lee : observations on not fitting
in / Paisley Rekdal.
        p.   cm.
    ISBN 0-375-40937-8
    1. Rekdal, Paisley. 2. Poets, American—20th century—Biography.
    3. Norwegian Americans—Social life and customs. 4. Chinese
    Americans—Social life and customs. 5. Asia—Description and
    travel. 6. Americans—Travel—Asia. I. Title.

    PS3568.E54 Z476 2000   811'.6—dc21   [B]   00-020636

Random House Web Address: www.randomhouse.com

Book design by Johanna Roebas

Printed in the United States of America
First Edition
9 8 7 6 5 4 3 2 1

To my parents, and to Eric

Contents

THE NIGHT
MY MOTHER
MET
BRUCE LEE

The Night My Mother
Met Bruce Lee

Age sixteen, my mother loads up red tubs of noodles, teacups chipped and white-gray as teeth, rice clumps that glue themselves to the plastic tub sides or dissolve and turn papery in the weak tea sloshing around the bottom. She's at Diamond Chan's restaurant, where most of her cousins work after school and during summer vacations, some of her friends, too. There's Suzy at the cash register, totaling up bills and giving back change, a little dish of toothpicks beside her and a basket of mints that taste like powdered cream. A couple of my mother's cousins are washing dishes behind the swinging kitchen door, and some woman called Auntie #2 (at her age, everyone is Auntie and each must take a number) takes orders at a table of women that look like Po Po's mah-jongg club. They don't play anymore. They go to the racetrack.

The interior of Diamond Chan's restaurant is red: red napkins, red walls, red carp in the tank and in signature seals on the

3

cheap wall hangings. Luck or no luck, it's like the inside of an esophagus. My mother's nails are cracked, kept short by clipping or gnawing, glisten only when varnished with the grease of someone else's leftovers. Still, she enjoys working here, its repetitive actions, the chores that keep her from thinking. The money my mother earns will soon get sucked into the price of a pink cashmere sweater for Po Po's birthday, along with a graduation photo of herself, also in a pink sweater, pearls, her face airbrushed fog-rose at the cheeks and mouth.

Graduation? Unlike her brothers, she knows she's going to college. Smith, to be exact, though without the approval of the school counselor. "Smith is . . . expensive," the school counselor told my mother only yesterday, which is why my mother is slightly irritated now, clomping around under the weight of full tubs of used dishes. "Smith is not for girls like you." What does she plan to be when she grows up? "A doctor?" my mother suggests. Um, no. "Nursing. Or teaching, perhaps, which is even more practical. Don't you think?"

My mother, who is practical above all things, agreed.

So it's the University of Washington in two years with a degree in education. Fine. She slams down full vials of soy sauce onto each table, makes sure the nozzle heads are screwed on exactly. Someone the other week stuck chewing gum up under the lid of one, and my mother had to dig it out with an old chopstick and then forgot to fully tighten the lid. Black, sweet-smelling pool on the white tablecloth. Seeing it, she could feel the back of her throat fill up with salt. Smith is not for girls like her.

"Cindy!" someone shouts. The kitchen door swings open. A momentary view: white chef shirts stained with red and brown grease. A woman wiping her brow with the back of her hand.

It is not, my mother would argue, the fact she could be denied the dream of Smith so much that someone should *tell* her she could be denied it. My mother knows the counselor was hinting at some limitation my mother would prefer to ignore. Still, she is whiter than white, should intelligence be considered a pale attribute. Deep down she understands she has a special capacity for work; she likes it, she's good at it, she excels at school and its predictable problems. Hers is a discipline entirely lacking in the spirits of whatever *loh fan* may sneer or wonder at her in study hall; to be told by a fat, dyed-blond guidance counselor she may be inferior? The monkey calling the man animal.

Now out of the kitchen erupts the newcomer, a smatter of duck fat and ash. Like everyone here, he's someone's cousin's cousin, though he talks like he's got marbles piled in his mouth.

"I come from Hong Kong," he told my mother on break in the alley. "From *real* Chinese." Is there a substitute? He leers at Suzy, waves his hand dismissively over the carved dragon beams, the waitresses gossiping in English. He's two years older than my mother, lean, high-cheekboned, shaggy-headed. He has big plans for himself. He likes to whip his arms and legs around in the kitchen, threaten the other busboy. Already he's dropped a dish, insulted the cook, cut his thumb on a knife blade. He smells funny.

"Mr. B. O. Jangles," Suzy calls him. "Kung Fooey."

"What the hell the matter with him?" growls Auntie #2. "I never seen nobody act like that before."

"It's all the rage in China," my mother says. She is repeating what he told her in a tone of voice that is meant to seem sarcastic but comes out another way. All the rage. In China.

She stacks more dishes in her tub. From the kitchen comes a high-pitched human squawk and the sound of something clatter-ing to the floor. He's going to get fired soon and my mother is never going to Smith. A waitress scurries out of the kitchen, bear-ing more food, a panicked look on her face. My mother stands and watches the kitchen door swing in place behind her. Back and forth, back and forth, back and forth.

Around age thirteen, for summer vacation I come down with laziness heretofore unheard of in a child. I doze in bed till noon at least, stay up every night watching bad movies or reading. Sometimes, if it's a bad enough movie and she is not teaching the next morning, my mother wakes and joins me.

Tonight is *Enter the Dragon*. I remember it because a year or two ago when it came out, all the boys on the block bought numchucks. We smacked our backs with the sticks on chains, left thumb-thick bruise prints on our rib cages. Jeff down the street still has the movie poster, still tells people he has a black belt in karate.

My mother and I watch Bruce Lee set foot on the island, followed closely by the playboy and the black man who will die after the banquet and all his women. Bruce Lee narrows his eyes, ripples his chest muscles underneath his white turtleneck.

"I knew him," my mother tells me. "I worked with him in a restaurant when I was in high school."

"Really?" This is now officially the only cool thing about her. "What was he like?"

"I don't remember. No one liked him, though. All that kung fu stuff; it looked ridiculous. Like a parody."

We watch in the dark as Bruce Lee confronts himself, over and over. In the hall of mirrors, his bloody chest and face seem outlined in silver. He is handsome and wiry; he caws at his opponents like an ethereal avenger. I peek at my mother beside me on the sofa. In the television light, her broad face twists into an expression I do not recognize. Then the light flickers, changes, makes her ordinary again.

One

WE DO NOT LIVE HERE, WE ARE ONLY VISITORS

We Do Not Live Here,
We Are Only Visitors

In Taipei one of the first things I notice are the white cotton masks strapped to the faces of the women. Men wear them, too, but the number of women wearing these makeshift face-filters exceed the number of men, and give Taipei the look of being run by a skinny, anonymous band of surgeons.

After two days my mother, who notices this as well, wants to buy a mask for herself. I argue against it more vehemently than the situation requires, saying that we will only be in Taipei twelve days; whatever damage meant to be done to our lungs in that time will not magically be eliminated by a piece of cotton with two rubber bands. But my mother insists. Near the markets where they sell the masks, she spends minutes haggling with the merchant for a better price than she believes she is being offered. I lounge and snort, tug her away when the merchant's gesticulations become too frenzied to be understood.

In restaurants we argue halfheartedly about the necessity of the masks until we reach a compromise. Now she walks around clutching an old scarf to her face and breathing shallowly. Soon we notice older Chinese women doing the same. Only the young women seem to have adopted the ear-band model. With my mother's wiry skunk hair and still-unlined almond eyes peeking over the tips of her scarf, she has the perfect outfit for traveling. Her brown scarf allows her to blend in with the crowds of older Chinese women in the markets and on the street while always covering her mouth, muffling the fact that she can't speak Chinese.

At night in Taipei after my mother dozes off in front of the hotel television, I think about Mark in Seattle, how we argue in bed together about whether we should marry. Mark had almost proposed twice but thought better of it, he said, when he recalled how easily I became seasick. Mark is an Englishman from Kent who works as a navigator for certain shipping companies. We met in Ireland, where I lived for a year; he followed me home when I returned to Seattle. Mark had half the year off from work and decided, in his typically spontaneous fashion, to buy a plane ticket to the States the morning he drove me to the airport. Within two weeks of my return he was sharing my room in the house I rented with friends.

Mark has hired himself out as a sailing instructor now and spends the better part of every weekend teaching his latest student the rudiments of tacking. I can't spend more than a few minutes on a boat without being overcome by nausea. Besides the fact of my seasickness, however, I have found other, more pressing reasons to be hesitant about marriage, such as our inability to agree on anything. Still, marriage seems like the next logical step we need to take in our relationship, and for a while we have pursued the subject relentlessly. But whatever reasons we could invent for ourselves to believe marriage is the right answer, neither of us makes a move to propose. We have stopped referring to marriage at all; my nausea has become a symbol of our stasis. "I'm going sailing," Mark will say, looking meaningfully at me. "Do you want to come?" And I, bilious at the sight of a dock, shake my head.

In the past weeks we have argued so much that we have stopped conversing almost altogether, replacing normal dialogue with sexual banter, teasing each other about our accents. "Zee-bra," I say. "Zeh-bra," Mark answers. Tonight in Taipei, in front of the flickering television, I think about his pink hands. The way his face always appears chapped in the sunset. I won't admit it to him, but I love his accent. The first time my maternal grandmother, Po Po, met him was at her birthday celebration at my parents' house in Seattle. "I can't understand a thing he says," she announced loudly after he'd greeted her.

In bed sometimes he asks me to recite the few Chinese phrases I know. "*Kai nooey,*" I say, stroking his chin. "*Gung hay fat choi. Shie shei. Soo jiep.*" But his favorite is the insult: the epithet Po Po called my father before my parents married.

"*Loh fan,*" I murmur, kissing him. "Old savage. *Loh fan.*"

In Taipei my mother asks about Mark. At first she didn't approve of my sleeping with him out of wedlock and, on their first meetings, had to mask her dislike of him on account of this with excessive politeness. My mother's politeness is terrifying. I've learned about this from ex-boyfriends who insist my mother is the most intimidating woman they have ever met; a single dinner once reduced a man named Tim to sweats and stutters. But when I confront her about this on a tour of the city, she acts playfully bemused.

"They're afraid of me?" She laughs. "I'm so nice."

"It's the niceness that's killing them. They think you're really pointing out their flaws."

"If their flaws are so obvious then I don't have to point them out, do I?" she asks. "It must be cultural. Politeness like that is very Chinese."

My mother has softened toward Mark since she suspects the relationship won't last. She gathers this from the number of times Mark and I fight, the days I've called her up, still yelling my side of the argument because Mark has stormed out of the house and stranded me with my anger. Any time we spend alone together, my mother feels free to question me so intimately that I have begun to suspect her concern really fronts some prurient desire to live through me vicariously. "Oh, you're just in this for the sex," she'll say, and then accuse me of innocence, of becoming steeped in the romantic tripe that has similarly ruined her generation of friends' marriages. To defend myself I try to dismantle my image as naïf as quickly and finally as possible by confessing the most embarrassing, cruel details of our couplehood; things I know I shouldn't tell her even as I reveal them, because if the relationship is going to lead to anything, some amount of privacy and trust has to be preserved. She knows this.

"You don't understand," I say.

"Oh, I do. You're fickle," she replies, and then demands to hear, yet again, how Mark drunkenly begged me to propose to him on New Year's and then, laughing, told me no. She tells me my boy-craziness is only exceeded by my gullibility when I tell her about the time I got so stoned I ended up in a corner and wouldn't leave until Mark, drunk himself, wrestled me out of my clothes and then left me there, naked. I embarrass myself, admitting these details. But I realize how proud my lack of loyalty to Mark makes me, how these secret transgressions increase my sense of independence. The more I tell my mother, the further apart I feel from him. "She wants to know," I tell myself. I feel like I can punish him.

By the seventh month of living with Mark, it was as if my mother had wormed her way into my skin, lodging there like a tick. Even now when Mark touches me after I spend a day alone with my mother, I become distant. I imagine she is there, bobbing above us along the ceiling. The next day the phone rings and I know it is her. I can hear her even before I pick up the receiver, her private ticking, how she is prepared to translate everything.

No one associates my mother and me with each other. To shop-keepers and hotel bellhops in Taipei we are two women traveling together, one white and one Chinese. Only when I address her as "Mom" within earshot of a Taiwanese is our situation made clear. "Your daughter?" he or she will stammer at this revelation, then I am scrutinized. I sometimes wonder what people make of our obvi-ous age discrepancy, how they would explain the older Chinese woman paying for the restaurant and hotel bills and clothes, what kind of relationship they could possibly expect between us. On the streets young women hold hands, cuddle, rest their heads on each other's shoulders. They walk arm in arm, like nineteenth-century couples, helping each other over puddles and curbs. My mother and I, when we travel, often walk like that together in public, where at home we would never think of doing it. In Taipei my mother takes my elbow at every corner (for my safety, not hers; she's fearless in traffic), runs her hand along my back in restau-rants or while waiting in long lines. Occasionally people look.

I don't blame the shopkeepers and bellhops for not immedi-ately understanding our relationship. My mother and I really don't look alike, though during the trip I begin to insist that we do. On

Christmas Eve, I stand beside her facing the hotel mirror as we make up our faces and say, "I have your nose."

"You do not have my nose," she replies, looking at me out of the corner of her eye.

"I do. Look, there's your nose."

"You don't look a thing like me."

"Mark says we have the same smile," I say, grinning widely to show her.

At this she snorts. "I don't think Mark sees you the way I see you."

"No, he sees me better. He's not as biased. Look," I say, and tilt my face so that its roundness becomes more apparent. "The same face."

"You look more like your father," she says then, ending the discussion. I can't argue with this. I do look more like my father— brown hair, narrow nose, even a chin that gently recedes in the same manner, though I do not have his light blue eyes and his broad shoulders. Still, I am taller than my mother, and thinner. Tonight, next to my mother in the mirror, I am struck by a sudden wave of vanity. I imagine that my face, next to hers, seems to glow. I pretend that my skin looks taut, my cheekbones sculpted. For those few imagined minutes my features are no longer a mark of oddity or Western exoticism, but of beauty. In this mirror I look more beautiful than my mother. And I feel strangely distant, cut off from her as if she were covered by a veil.

On the street people stare at me, but not because I am beautiful. Taipei is not populated with hordes of white Westerners like Tokyo or Hong Kong. Here I am scrutinized, though politely, by passersby. They do not, I believe, ever recognize that I am half Chinese. They do not realize that my mother and I know each other. I walk quickly while my mother tends to shuffle; ten minutes into any walk my mother ends up six feet or more behind me. No one, unless they suspect that she is my handservant (as my mother jokes), would place the Chinese matron with the white girl.

Watching my mother in shopwindows, I see her round smooth face with the curls of permed hair, the thicker lips and wide nose. I remember the childhood friend who visited my home and met her for the first time. "What is your mother?" he had asked in private afterward. He did not, I notice, ask the same question about me.

Appearance is the deciding factor of one's ethnicity, I understand; how I look to the majority of people determines how I should behave and what I should accept to be my primary culture. This is not simply a reaction white America has to race. If for the past several years I have become a part of white America it is because it has embraced me so fully, because it is everywhere, because it is comfortable to disappear into, and because the Chinese would not recognize me on sight. Any struggle to assert myself as more than what I seem to be is exhausting. A choice, I realized, either could be made by me or asserted for me. Alone in the bathroom, I plucked my thick Asian eyebrows down to niggling scrubs and watched my brown eyes grow wide in my face, less hooded, more Italian-looking.

Only when I am shown photos of myself and see the new frozen images of me, the overplucked brows and insincere half-smile slapped onto my face, do I become disturbed. Only when I say, "I'm sure I don't look like that," and my friends agree—"No, you don't look like that in real life, you look very different"—does it occur to me what façade I am staring at. What digs at me so painfully when I see myself.

We are not visiting relatives in this country. We are visiting over the Christmas holidays, we tell strangers who ask, and we know no one in all of Taipei.

In shops my mother pretends she understands the salespeople when they speak to her. But even if she knew as much Mandarin as Cantonese, there is no way she could translate a sentence spoken by a Taiwanese six-year-old, let alone the murderously fast speech of an adult.

In Sogo Department Store, a young saleswoman with spidery eyebrows approaches my mother by a rack of sweaters. The girl wears a black tunic over a white shirt and black stockings. She barely lifts her feet when she walks: what my mother calls "the Chinese shuffle." She notices my mother fingering the material of a red sweater and immediately pounces on the garment's tag, lecturing, I suppose, on its exact blend and weave. I am guessing she tells my mother about how cool it will be for summer. My mother nods and grunts, lets escape a few of the guttural "Ahs" that have begun to punctuate her speech in Taiwan. Suddenly, I realize where she has picked this up; behind me two women converse about the merits of a handbag, and when one speaks, the other replies by fiercely grunting "Ah." My mother is mimicking her.

"Mom," I say, pointing to my watch. The salesgirl turns to me and narrows her eyes. She looks from my mother to me, the sweater dangling from her fingers. She continues speaking to my mother in Chinese though it is obvious that my mother does not know what she is talking about and that the salesgirl, like the signature seal–makers and waitresses before her, is merely babbling to herself. The salesgirl stops and clears her throat. I come forward to stand by my mother's side.

"Where are you from?" she asks in English.

"Washington. Seattle," my mother replies. She looks at me.

"Your daughter?" the salesgirl manages to get out. "She is very . . . tall." Then she walks away.

"Mom," I say later, at a restaurant for lunch, "you shouldn't do that."

"It's rude to tell her I speak English."

"It's rude to let her go on like that."

"I can understand some things she says," my mother says defensively. But she doesn't really. I can tell by her blank expression and fierce, repetitive "Ahs" during these moments that she's simply trying to cover up.

"She wasn't speaking Cantonese."

"I meant I understood her gestures."

We sit at the dim sum restaurant in silence. My mother has successfully ordered in Chinese, but when the dishes come they are the same dishes we eat in Seattle with Po Po and the same ones we ate yesterday and the day before. I suddenly realize that my mother has been ordering only the foods whose names she knows. On the plane she had declared that she would eat dog before we left, but I can see, with a mixture of disappointment and relief, that this is a prophecy that will not come true. My mother doesn't know the word "dog" in Chinese. Tonight we pick at our food while planning our next day together and I tell her, again, how much I love oyster hash.

When Mark asks about my family, he is relieved to learn that not only I, but my mother and my mother's mother, were all born in Washington State. "Oh," he says. "That's different."

The history of my family is complicated and vaguely dangerous, as my Aunt Opal insinuates through long looks and abrupt silences at the dinner table. There is something about a tong war, sudden deaths, a disease that couldn't be cured by anything but a special herb that grows only in Canton. The patriarch was dying and the family split up its members into separate households, sending one child, Aunt Opal, to New York and my grandmother to Hong Kong at age nine. Po Po didn't return to Seattle till she was almost twenty. For those eleven years she was actually Chinese, though the entire time, she insists, she dreamed of eating bread by the fistfuls. And she is still, according to both Chinese and American standards regarding race, really Chinese where my mother and I might seem to be impostors. She possesses the homogeneity of physical appearance (the same black hair and eyes, her body perhaps a little stouter than the bodies of the Taiwanese from all the bad American food) and cultural values. She understands the appropriate Chinese rules regarding rudeness and civility so ruthlessly employed by waitresses across Taiwan. Po Po married Chinese. Her body stayed faithful. My mother's and mine do not.

In Seattle, Mark longed for sailing harbors and a good bar, "a real pub," he said once, where he could get Newcastle beer. For two weeks last month we went out every night to a different bar by the water where we would sit and drink pints of lager in silence until I got drunk or Mark tired of the atmosphere and the poor quality of the beer. Then we would go home, fall asleep, and wake the next morning planning for another evening out.

One day, before my mother and I bought tickets to Taiwan, I learned of a disturbing rumor at my college. Several members of the English department felt that the prevailing tone of the university was elitist; people had begun to band in camps of friends that somewhat depended on race and racial sympathies. When I arrived as a student I was not aware of the friction, nor was I close friends with any of the other mixed students in my department, of whom there were only three, at the time. One evening a biracial Latina woman invited me to a dinner party which I could not attend because I was ill. Then I learned of the theory circulating about my absence that night: I was ashamed of being half Chinese. The day I found out about this I met Mark late in the evening at the Blue Unicorn, where he was already working on his third can of Guinness.

"What a load of trash," he said when I told him.

"I don't know how to act now," I said.

"There's nothing to act about. They go around making such a big stink when it doesn't even matter. Half my family comes from France for God's sakes and I don't care."

"I don't think the Norman conquest counts, Mark."

"Then what does count? You don't look Chinese and you don't speak Chinese. At least I can read French."

"Which you learned in school."

"Your mother doesn't speak Chinese," he said, pushing his chair back.

"This is different."

"How is this different?" he demanded, but I couldn't say.

Later I could articulate the differences between us by telling him that my mother, because of her round and slightly sallow face, her dark hair and eyes, would always be perceived as Asian first. Regardless of her fluency in English, my mother's appearance allows her to be categorized, her experience isolated from that of white America, to be discriminated against in the worst situations. No one in England could simply point to Mark's mother or grandmother and say "French" on first sight. Not without being told.

But at the bar I couldn't articulate any of this because I was recalling something further back, a conversation at my parents' home after dinner when my mother had questioned my father and me about what we might change about our lives had we the opportunity. That night she had surprised us by making a pitcher of margaritas, which we drank during the course of the meal. My mother rarely drinks and hates it when my father consumes more than two martinis at a go. For years she refused to serve alcohol at the house when I visited. "I don't want to condone a bad habit," she had said. "I don't want to be blamed if you become an alcoholic."

"Tell me," she insisted that evening. And, irritated, slightly drunk, I told her I wouldn't want to be half Chinese.

"Full or nothing," I said.

"Fully what?" she asked.

"Whatever," I had replied.

"The fact is, it isn't different," Mark finished and stood to get another beer. "If you married me not one person in England would think you were half Chinese. You want to be different and so you make it a difference." When the waiter came to take his order, he sat back down again, fumbling for his money.

After the bar we went home in a cab which Mark paid for. He told me that his company had started sending letters to the officers in England; soon Mark's year-long vacation would end and he'd go back to sea. I could see this delighted him and, even though I was still angry, kissed him for congratulations.

That night in bed he tugged my long hair back with his fingers, holding it in place while he fumbled on the nightstand for my hair clip.

"We have to decide what we'll do," I said.

"About the apartment?"

"About staying together."

He brought his lips close to my temples. "I can't afford to get married now," he said.

"I'm not sure I want to get married."

"Fine," he replied.

"Fine," I said. He leaned into me then and his collarbone smelled of lager. "You really should wear your hair back more," he whispered. "You look like a little China doll like that."

When his smell grew too much to stand I sat up violently in bed, pushing him away.

At the National Gallery my mother turns to me in front of the jade cabbage display and announces, "I hope you won't marry Mark."

I had been talking somewhat along the same lines myself the past few days, but it surprises me to hear her say it.

"What don't you like about him?" I ask, and she looks at me.

"He doesn't read, doesn't think, doesn't treat you well," she says. "Doesn't like to do anything but sail and you get sick on boats . . ."

I recalled what Po Po had said the first time I mentioned him.

"It's serious, Po Po," I said. "He's coming from England to visit me."

"Is he white?" she asked.

"Yes," I said.

"That's too bad."

". . . doesn't even think he's in love with you . . ."

"I didn't say that," I say suddenly. "I never said that."

We stop beside a display of ivory miniatures, a tiny woman with white sleeves on a mountain. In the distance lurked a tiger.

"Did Po Po ever tell you not to marry Dad?" I ask.

"Of course not," she says, and I know Po Po didn't have to; my grandmother had refused to speak to my mother when she told her.

"Why do you ask me such embarrassing things?" I demanded.

"What things?"

"You're always asking about our sex life," I say, and my mother's left eye narrows because she can sense we are being watched, overheard, though probably not understood.

"I never ask," she hisses. "You misunderstand my questions."

I walk in frustrated silence for several minutes while she comments glibly about the thousand tiny wood Buddhas stacked in rows, each carving made anonymous by the fact of so many others. "I just don't understand why you don't like him," I say.

"He exoticizes you," she says finally. "If you want to marry him," she continues, "fine. You can ruin your life with mistakes. After all it doesn't matter what I think about him, it's what you think that makes the difference."

"You just hate him because he's white," I say. She snorts and shakes her head. But her lips close together tightly, as if she is chewing on their delicate inner skin, and I know this is true. In Taipei and at home whenever we see white men with Asian women my mother grimaces complicitously in my direction. I know what she is thinking: *This man is taking advantage of her because she is Chinese.*

It occurs to me now to ask her if she despises my father—the man who had known her for ten years and shyly courted her through college—for loving her, if indeed he does take advantage of her in private because she is Chinese. But I know he doesn't mistreat her; my mother is not docile or shy or subservient. She does not wait to speak until spoken to and she never kowtows. My father is the silent partner in their marriage, the one always trailing a few steps behind.

"Are you sorry you didn't marry Chinese?" I ask.

"What has that got to do with anything?"

"Are you sorry that I'm half?"

"What are you taking about?" she asks angrily, but I can tell that she understands. How much more Chinese we both would have been, I think bitterly, had she married within the community.

I feel like the salesgirl in Sogo with the spidery eyebrows, cheap sweater dangling between my fingers. I can see her fully now; I suddenly understand what she's saying. I have finally been let into the secret.

———

We've been arguing the whole day: where north is, the best café for tea. This is the third overcast day and my mother, who packed for warmer weather, is wrapped in a thick sweatshirt she had to buy in order to keep warm. Bundled up this way, it's hard to recognize her in stores or museums. Her appearance makes her anonymous. "I'm freezing," she repeats in the hotel lobby, and I shrug exasperatedly.

It is our next-to-last afternoon in Taipei, and I realize I haven't sent anyone a postcard. Dutifully, I trundle out to the local shop to buy a fistful of cards and can't think of what to write. There is very little that is immediately beautiful about Taipei—only by poring over a map and finding spots like university parks and relatively unvisited temples have we discovered any color, any ornamental relief in this city dominated by high-rises and desolate-looking pockets of houses. Beside the hotel stands a tenement with every window lined with laundry. I keep track of the window toward the far east side, fifth story. Every morning the laundry is different. Today it's four shirts, each white, and a pair of pink shorts. I imagine the woman coming home every night from work and selecting a small portion of the huge laundry pile she must do for the evening. She believes in working in increments; she imagines that by doing just a little every day she can overcome this massive load, never admitting to herself that in a single day she dirties as much as she cleans in a night and so is always stuck in the same place come morning.

When I reach Mark's postcard I can't think of what to write that doesn't sound false or irrelevant. In the end I print, "I'll miss you"; send it, unsigned, from the hotel postbox.

———

On our last day in Taipei, we both develop hacking coughs that we suspect have more to do with the excessive pollution than the slight flu I caught. To celebrate the end of our vacation I teasingly suggest to Mom that we buy ourselves cotton masks. She glares at me. "Part of growing up," she says, "is learning when to drop it." But we still have to get gifts for family and so we make our way to the market. On the way we find a shop specializing in Thai silks and tablecloths. We go in.

The woman running the shop looks like she'd once spent a significant amount of time in her life following the Grateful Dead. Black bangs completely cover her eyes and she walks around the shop barefoot. Three thick silver bangles slide up and down her tiny arms, covering, the woman insists, "her hideous wrists." My mother and I, sick of each other's company, part immediately at the entrance of the shop, and I go and plant myself in a corner where the saleswoman has stacked ready-made dresses.

My mother fingers everything. The saleswoman speaks rapid-fire Chinese which my mother grunts at, then, guessing that my mother doesn't really understand her, begins typing the prices up on a calculator she has at hand and listing off bits of information in English. I am glad she's caught on to my mother; when their backs are turned I smirk appreciatively at my mother's flustered gestures.

Suddenly my mother turns to me, a full amber-colored cloth draped over her hands. "What do you think?" she asks.

I go over and touch it. "It's beautiful," I say. "How much?"

The saleswoman taps the price into the calculator.

"Buy it," I say.

My mother nods and the woman shuffles off, her patchwork skirt swinging across her feet.

"Visit family here?" she asks as she packs the cloth in paper and I shake my head. We have no family in Taiwan. We know no one in this whole city. She glances over to where my mother sits, hugging herself for warmth. "Your mother?" she asks blandly as I step forward to receive the wrapped package for my mother.

"Yes," I say slowly. The saleswoman nods.

"Different faces, same feelings," she says. My mother coughs and I smile too broadly.

We decide to pretend she is right.

Two

OTHER
WOMEN

Americans Abroad

When I was twenty I thought I knew something about Japanese art. I liked it, which I thought meant I must inherently understand it. So in college I applied for and received a scholarship to stay with two families in the seaport town of Kobe for the summer—my first trip out of the country. In my application I wrote that I was interested in Japanese aesthetics, a suggestion inspired by my mother. She thought it would be a good idea for me to see other countries China had influenced; to see, if indirectly, my culture. But in Japan I could find only postcards of the art I liked—woodblock prints from the nineteenth century—and bought them in packets at tourist sites. I purchased postcards of sumo wrestlers and bath scenes, part of a man's dun-colored face peeking through a break in the wood screen of a woman's bath. I loved their look and design. "So traditional!" I told my host sister Hiroko, who disliked them and sent them to friends in America.

When I arrived in Japan, Hiroko seemed nonplussed that I preferred buying postcards to taking actual photographs with her of the places we saw. Hiroko was my age and studied English at a local Kobe community college or university—I was never sure which in her translation—before planning to take a job as a bank manager. We liked each other. She had a younger sister named Junko with large, mournful eyes and a perpetual pout which belied her tendency to find everything around her absurd. Their parents were shy and solicitous. Only Hiroko spoke English. Without her, the family and I made hand gestures or I spoke the limited Japanese I picked up in conversation and furiously copied into a school notebook to memorize.

Hiroko's family lived in a narrow, peach-colored house built in an emerging network of exact replicas several miles out from the Kobe city center. A few sparse trees peppered the neighborhood, but there was almost no grass, even on the small playground with its steel merry-go-round. Outside Hiroko's house a few plants struggled to survive in large black-glazed pots; the entranceway was too small to have a proper garden. Inside the house everything appeared to have been painted pink or lemon and looked new. There were stuffed animals in the bedrooms and on the chairs, a puffy tan leatherette couch, and Hello Kitty–style ornaments stacked on the kitchen shelves and on top of bookcases. Even the kitchen appliances were plastic and adorable, full of perky bleeps and coos. The only traditional ornaments were found in a side room done with tatami and decorated simply with one or two Japanese calligraphy scrolls, a low wood teak table and black pillows stacked neatly in the corner. We used the room to eat suki-yaki in.

Whenever I bought a Japanese woodblock postcard Hiroko would look at me and shrug. "OK," she would say doubtfully. She trudged through the large wooden temples and dark blue and white palaces alongside me, lit up at my interest in shopping malls or the inscrutable pachinko parlors with their eye-blistering neon interiors. She liked teaching me Japanese but seemed more interested in having me speak English, which she would repeat back in loud, excited gasps. She had a smoky man's voice that would rise instantly to a wisp on the telephone or before strangers. She was cheerful, brusque, practical, but she liked teaching me children's songs and origami, and she loved driving me to places where she knew there wouldn't be white people. One time she took me to her old grade school and told me to wander the halls while she spoke to a teacher who worked there. Within minutes the windows and doorways filled with white-shirted children shouting and jumping for my attention. Hiroko came barreling down the hallway toward me, grinning, with her camera.

Before Kobe, I had visions of Japanese gardens from the Arboretum's replica in Seattle, their furlike mosses, the miniature trees bound to choking with coils of copper wire. At home I had imagined the stately shoguns' fortresses and how the black wood floors would creak when I paced between glassed displays of old weaponry, what meals I would eat in the spare long rooms covered with tatami: a little rice, clear fish soup. My first morning with Hiroko, I awoke from a dream of sliding screens to toast made from enormous slices of bread, spread thickly with peanut butter and pieces of banana. Next to the plate was a small carton of whole milk so rich it tasted like cream. I ate it all to be polite but the next morning there it was again. Again I gagged down the pillowy bread, the banana chunks smothered with greasy peanut butter. The third morning I couldn't stand it. "I can't eat this," I apologized to Hiroko.

"Americans don't eat this?" she asked, pointing at the peanut butter.

"Maybe Elvis," I said.

She thought for a moment. "Have some soup," she hesitantly replied.

Hiroko's family put a lot of work into figuring out what I could eat. They owned a small, slightly dingy sushi shop near a train station and were afraid I would hate the taste of raw fish and cold rice. They were delighted to find I knew the names of the different sushi already: futomaki, ebi, toro. Relieved, they fed me slice after slice, brought home whole platters of braised eel and tuna rolls, salmon roe. They spent a fortune feeding me, trying out all the different delicacies at first out of sheer relief, then out of an interest to discover just where my American palate must kick in. They served raw, painfully rubbery clams that sounded like gravel when chewed; barley tea drunk cold; brown puddles of fermented soybeans that looked like strings of dog saliva. Once a live little fish. I loved this family. I loved Junko and Hiroko, who sat and played board games in Japanese with me and laughed and laughed and laughed. I loved them so much I ate everything, I couldn't stop. They watched me dip yards of buckwheat noodles and cabbage into a bowl of raw egg yolk, holding their breaths. But it was easy for me to choke down the translucent squid legs, to peel the perfumed skins off the tiny black grapes with my teeth. I smiled at them and licked the brown natto off my chopsticks, string by greasy string.

I had become an aggressive eater, if not an intelligent one; at one scholarship meeting I once enthusiastically ate some table decorations. I had done it after a Japanese businessman had sidled up to ask me, in his best English, what I thought about America's declining position in the world. How did I feel knowing children in Arkansas were growing so fat they couldn't move from their couches? I shook my head politely and kept eating. Down the lethal green wasabi mound; each slick petal of ginger, pink as pickled skin. Then the tiny gold and purple flower garnishes scattered around my bento box. I popped one, two, three, into my mouth, chewing vigorously before someone, whispering, could inform me that these weren't delicacies.

One night Hiroko and her family invited her widowed grandfather over for dinner. He was curious about me and questioned me relentlessly through Hiroko. "We still love America," he assured me. "Americans brought us everything to survive after the war. If it wasn't for the Americans, Japan would be nothing." We sped by the outskirts of Kobe in the white family Isuzu. The grandfather sat in the front seat of the car. He had a round head and skin that appeared rubbery, completely white hair, thick glasses. It was raining, I recall, and every time he turned his head to speak to me, the flashing windshield wipers looked like they rocketed out of his almost too-pink ear. Did America hate Japan for becoming too successful? he wanted to know. Did America feel shame for what had happened to it?

After dinner Hiroko and her family left the grandfather and me alone while they brought out dessert. The grandfather smiled kindly. He had a large, owlish face made comical by the fact a bee had stung his upper lip while he'd been gardening. The lip was eggplant-colored now, swollen and tight as if the skin could barely contain what lay behind it. "I look like a duck," he'd chuckled. Alone with me in the family living room he touched his upper lip gingerly with his tongue and asked me a question in Japanese I don't know how I understood with my basic grammar.

What do they call this in America? he asked. I looked down. He had unzipped his pants and pulled out his penis, which looked bulky, a dull olive-pink tinged with dusky purple resembling his lip.

"Pathetic?" I replied brightly in English. He smiled and pushed the candy dish toward me. I coughed politely. I sucked on the small, sour candies.

Hiroko wanted to learn about America in school, so she purchased an English textbook that compared the educational styles of Japanese, Chinese and American kindergartens. "Chinese are worst," she informed me, offering me the book to read. "America is the best; Japan has many problems to make children original."

"I'll read it," I replied.

"We have heard that about Japan: that we are not original. What do you think about Japan?"

"In America? That you're creative enough to make everything cheaper and better." It was 1991, and for the last few years the only international news from Asia seemed to be about Japan—its car industry, its technology, its problems with trade. In their ability to push themselves in work they were, almost, a society of automatons, suggested one business article my father had clipped from a magazine and given me before my trip. Almost ruthless.

"That's pretty original," I told her.

"Yes, but fruit is expensive in Japan."

I wasn't sure how this related but didn't ask.

She watched me with her black eyes. She started giggling as I pantomimed American children in kindergarten. I pretended to pick my nose and wail for the teacher and sulk. She loved it when I performed for her and called me "Mr. Bean."

I didn't confess to Hiroko, when she continued to ask what I thought of Japan, about the movies I had watched in preparation for my trip. Over the course of a few weeks I had read *The Tale of Genji* and countless haiku, and had even fought my way partly through a dry history of Japan from my father's bookcase that turned me narcoleptic. After that I decided film might be the best way to prepare, and rented a series of Japanese horror movies and one black-and-white art drama that turned out to be pornographic.

I remember only the end scene, in which the man and woman make love, coming to simultaneous orgasm only when the woman strangles the man to death with a piece of rope. The next day I was eating dinner with my parents and Po Po when I mentioned the films.

"Kurosawa?" my mother asked.

"Not exactly," I replied.

My mother looked at me. I already knew what my answer should have been. My mother was very positive about Japanese culture these days. In fact she had become positive about anything Asian, out of some dubious sense of fraternity. She had once tried to dispel the stereotype of the Japanese being "unoriginal" in a government grant application for her school district by pasting little pictures of lightbulbs over drawings of samurai's heads. The grant was to educate students about Japanese history in the Seattle schools. It was denied.

"I'm sure it was good," my mother said, answering for me instead. "Japan was years ahead of the Americans when it came to movies, you know. They still are. You *must* have liked it."

"Well," I replied, "it was entertaining. But it wasn't very good."

"Of course it wasn't," Po Po cut in loudly, dropping a gnawed porkchop bone onto her plate with a splash of grease. "It was Japanese!"

My mother rolled her eyes over Po Po's head as she placed a bowl of green beans down before us. "Have a good trip," she warned me.

"'Hey Jude' is an English song, you sing that," the director of the scholarship program told us. They had gathered all the students together for our first banquet. Since we had eaten, it was time for the entertainment. We were scheduled to perform.

"I don't think the Swedes know that song," a girl from Kansas suggested hopefully.

"Of course we do!" huffed one of the Swedes. The Kansas girl's face fell.

"Well, maybe the Italian then. She doesn't know it."

"Everyone knows 'Hey Jude,'" the director insisted. "You are Americans abroad!" The Italian and the Swedes glared at him. The director was a tall, very slender Chinese man who had moved to Japan, opened several restaurants and taught himself English solely with the aid of cassette tapes. Because of this he spoke in a slightly mechanical way, with the broad, overemphasized tones of a California game show host. He hated the Korean exchange students on our program for "cultural" reasons, but liked the Americans because he could use at inappropriate moments the slang expressions he had learned on cassette. "That's a-*maze*-ing!" he had cried when one of the Danish students spilled miso soup down the front of her blouse.

"Does the Italian know it?"

"I don't care," the Italian sulked. "I sing anything."

"Good! Fun! You sing 'Hey Jude.'" The director beamed and ushered us onto the stage. We stood, fifteen Americans, seven Canadians, four Swedes, three Danes, three Koreans and the Italian, and proceeded to sing. After about five minutes, the Japanese businessmen at the banquet looked Novacained.

"Nah-nah-nah-nah," droned the Swedes at the karaoke screen. The Italian sighed dramatically and looked like she hated us all.

"A-*maze*-ing!" cried the director.

Back at the tables to pour drinks for the Japanese men, the scholarship students smiled politely as the businessmen asked after our nationalities. "I'm American," I told one portly man. He wore a dark blue suit and thin blue socks through which his white foot skin gleamed. "But I'm half Chinese," I added. I told him this belligerently, desperate to get out of my next singing engagement: a solo rendition of "You Are My Sunshine." I wanted somehow to ally myself with him, his place in the audience drinking beer and watching others perform. *I'm like you*, I silently begged. *Save me from my culture.*

"American," he replied. "It is too bad what is happening to your country." He drained the glass I had poured for him, then poured me a Coke to drink. When I finished my own glass he laughed as if he'd made a joke, but he stared at me too long while doing it and eased his fingers slowly onto my bare forearm. They tapped just above my wrist throughout the next act the Canadians sang alone, "Rocky Mountain High." He kept along with them, stiffly, in time.

In July, all the homestay students changed families. Hiroko led me to the crowded Kobe train station where she was to hand me and my luggage off to my next parents. A swirl of foreign students looked nervously at the empty platform. Junko and I were exchanging teary address cards in the parking lot when a white car lunged to a halt beside us and a large, egg-shaped man jumped out. His other four family members exited afterward, less enthusiastically.

"We welcome you," the egg-shaped man, Mr. Tanaka, announced. He grabbed my hand and began pumping it furiously. His upper body snapped into an eager bow. Behind him I could make out a well-dressed girl who I assumed was his daughter. She looked me up and down and smiled unconvincingly. Her brother, beside her, scowled.

My father's business article had included a short profile of what its author considered the average Japanese family, which I had cursorily dismissed, but, after spending a week with the

Tanakas, I was struck by how cannily similar the description was to my new host family. Here was the long-waisted, nervous mother, the hard-drinking father who ignored her, the studious and miserable children. Like Hiroko's family, the Tanakas were unfailingly kind, but they seemed awkward with each other, and I blamed this fact on my presence in their house: a potentially disastrous responsibility. For instance, Mr. Tanaka, who looked distressingly like Homer Simpson, became obsessed with my bowel movements. Every morning at breakfast he asked in his ponderous English whether the Japanese diet "agreed" with me. "Some people do not go to the bathroom," he murmured. "They stop . . . you understand?"

"I'm OK," I replied, and went back to eating maniacally.

The Tanakas had air-conditioning, a rarity in Japanese homes, and a large walled-in garden. The rooms in the house had high ceilings and matching dark wood furniture. The family worked at their two enormous, brightly lit kimono shops that kept both husband and wife busy late into the evening.

My translators were Mr. Tanaka and his lovely daughter, Fumiko. There was an older brother away at college who, the family insisted, was fluent in English, but he was too busy working this summer to meet me. Instead, Fumiko would act as my guide. Fumiko had sleepy, double-lidded eyes and a thick wash of hair she French-braided or pinned back, letting her bangs sweep gently down into her eyelashes. Her brother, Takeyoshi, was slender and had his father's slightly bug eyes and permanently startled expression. He was seventeen and just learning to drive a motor scooter when I arrived, and there were many frantic conversations in Japanese that exploded between the family members whenever he suggested he take me out for a ride. Mrs. Tanaka, a plump woman with permed hair, seemed permanently to be wringing her hands at the sight of me. "Oh, oh, oh," she would begin every sentence in

English. Then she would give up, motioning for one of the children to come and rescue her.

The Tanakas also had the father's mother living with them in the same house. The Tanaka grandmother was a short, squat woman with dyed-black hair and glasses with lenses the shape of small tea saucers. She bullied everyone in the house, cooked or cleaned constantly, and did not seem embarrassed at all by the fact I did not speak Japanese. Whenever I was left alone in the house with her she would talk to me in a steady, voluble stream of Japanese, handing me brush or rag or vacuum cleaner, whatever she wanted me to clean with. I was grateful, having something to do with my hands. She also enjoyed complaining about her left leg, gripping her knee or shin with one hand and pointing to it with the other, muttering bitterly. Before I left I gave her the thousand cranes I'd been folding as an experiment in origami; Hiroko had taught me and made several hundred herself. I gave them to the grandmother after learning that a thousand cranes are believed to solve medical problems as well as grant wishes. The grandmother cried softly for a few minutes after I gave them to her, then ordered me back into the living room with the vacuum.

I knew Fumiko and I were meant to be partners during my stay, possibly best friends. Mr. Tanaka chauffeured us to her tea ceremony and ikebana classes, to shopping malls and shakuhatchi concerts, but we didn't like each other. Fumiko dressed in girlish designer clothes and spoke in a soft high voice I mistrusted instinctively. She wore little Chanel earrings and a soft dusting of perfume on both wrists. To my great amusement, she also had a boyfriend with an American-style bomber jacket with the English flag sewn onto the back. He showed up with T-shirts and jeans emblazoned with English phrases like "Waves Driffing to the Sea," "Happy Big America School" and "Raging Zit." He nodded at me but spoke, rarely, through Fumiko. Fumiko preferred the

Japanese-American girls she had met at the scholarship meetings instead, and, jealously, I watched her cry over one girl who left early on a flight back to San Francisco. Fumiko would not cry over me, I knew. I had broken out in heat rash, was irascible, did not like wearing face powder in the summer. Fumiko blinked and blinked at me, watching my face greasily contort in the humidity.

"She eats a lot," I heard her say to her father one night, and pretended not to understand. "She eats like a *man.*" The brother said something incomprehensible and Mr. Tanaka chuckled a deeply nervous chuckle. *Oh, it's fine,* I imagined him saying. *Maybe it will help her take a dump.* Instead of replying he turned on the TV, adjusted the controls so that an American movie—a remake of *The Blob*—could be played in English.

"Can you get all American movies in English?" I asked Fumiko.

"Yes," she said. "If the station says so."

"Why?"

"So we learn English." This came from a sullen Takeyoshi. He sounded bored and slightly disgusted. I tried to sympathize.

"Japanese is a popular language to study in America," I said politely, channeling my mother. "Everyone wants to know it."

"They must," he replied through Fumiko.

"My grandmother didn't teach my mother Chinese because she thought English was more important," I tried again.

Fumiko's brother snorted and went back to examining the movie. He and his sister watched until they grew bored, then they went silently to their separate rooms.

But later, when Fumiko showed me—yet again—how to use their Japanese bathtub, she picked up on the topic. "You are American," Fumiko began.

"Yes."

"So you speak English."

"Right."

"So your mother speaks English."

"Yes. But she also could speak Chinese."

"No, she can't."

"Yes, actually, she could."

"She is American."

"Yes, she is American."

"So she speaks English."

I paused, waiting for the conversation to get more interesting.

"Yes, and she could have spoken Chinese if her mother taught her," I argued politely again, realizing it wouldn't.

"But she couldn't teach her. She is American."

"But she is also Chinese."

"No, she's American."

"She's Chinese-American. I'm half Chinese. I'm American, but I'm also part Chinese."

Fumiko narrowed her eyes as she looked at me. "No," she said again. "I am sorry, but you are American."

"OK. You got me. I'm American," I said.

"And you must speak English," she said.

"I do," I told her, bewildered. "I'm speaking it all the time."

"My father does not want you to speak Japanese," she explained. "You write down," she said, pretending to scribble words in an invisible notebook, "and you speak. He wants you to speak English to us."

"I do speak English to you."

"Always," she said brusquely.

"Always," I repeated.

I stood at the entrance of the bathroom and thought about Fumiko and the Japanese-American girl at the airport, how Fumiko had dabbed at the corners of her eyes with an embroidered handkerchief as the girl disappeared down the gangway.

"If Sara spoke Japanese," I said, referring to the Japanese-American, "would you speak Japanese back?"

"Perhaps," she said. "But my father wants you to speak English so we speak English. He wants us to know more. Please speak English." She did not say this in a pleading tone of voice. She twisted the delicate pearl and diamond necklace tightly around her neck with a finger as she waited for my agreement. When she got it, she nodded good night to me and went to her room to call her boyfriend. I knew, though she hadn't told me, that they were going to an American-style dance club the next night with friends. I planned to stay home. I didn't have to ask. I already knew that their evening would be private.

Mr. Tanaka discovered I loved traditional Japanese dancing, and so we attended all the Bon Odori festivals across Kobe and Osaka, me dressed in a blue yukata covered in multicolored flowers and butterflies, so that I could dance. The Japanese dances were simple, elegant, almost mathematical in their precision. I would join a large circle of Japanese men and women in yukatas as they wound their way slowly around a raised wooden platform on which a drummer beat time. The drum was surrounded by four older Japanese women in black and white yukatas who demonstrated the dance the rest of us were to follow. If I got lost or forgot the movements, I watched the women on the platform. But the dances were simple to pick up. I dipped gently and bowed in time, swung my hands in easy circles to the drum. Mr. Tanaka stood on the sidelines with Fumiko, who wore a pink yukata she didn't like, and watched.

"You like?" he asked when I left the line of Japanese dancers. My back was warm and damp under my yukata.

"I love it!" I replied, looking for something to drink.

"Then dance more!" He ushered me back into the line of dancers. That night he worried so much about my love of dancing that he wouldn't let me sit down. If he saw me edge toward a seat he would quickly hustle me back into the line, crying, "You like to dance? Dance!" This soon became our ritual: when as we got to any festival he would rush me toward the stage, herding me into any dance line where I would spend all our time there moving around and around in a circle. When I passed him, I could see him pointing me out to strangers or acquaintances, handing out business cards.

"He wants you to like Japan," Fumiko said. "He wants you to like everything Japanese."

"I do," I muttered.

"He says you are unusual because Americans cannot do Japanese dances."

"That's true. Americans don't learn Japanese dances."

"Americans cannot do Japanese dances."

"They don't *know* Japanese dances," I said. "They could do them if they learned."

Fumiko looked confused. "But Americans cannot do Japanese dances," she insisted. "They are Japanese-style, not American-style."

I could feel a headache percolating in my brain. "It's a dance," I said. "You learn it by imitating it."

"You can't imitate."

"So I'm not dancing Japanese-style?"

"Yes, you are not dancing Japanese-style."

"It's not correct?"

"Yes, it is not correct."

"What?"

"What?"

We stared at each other. "I have to sit down," I told Fumiko. "I need to let my head finish exploding."

"Would you like to take a goldfish?" she replied.

I looked up at her. She smiled and waved her wide pink sleeve in the direction of some children crouched around a red plastic tub of water. They were playing a game, I could see, in which the participants each clutched a little wire handle with a scoop covered with a membrane of rice paper. As the children thrust the scoop under the water to catch a goldfish, the paper weakened. The point was to catch a fish with the scoop without the paper tearing. Fumiko smiled as she led me over. She paid for me and watched.

She laughed for the first time that evening, watching my fish break through the soaked paper, my scoop dipping and dipping uselessly after it.

I missed Hiroko and Junko, often thought about calling them from the Tanakas, but the phone was difficult for me to use and, when I did succeed in calling the sisters, communication between us was strained. We needed to see one another to understand what we were saying. Still, I wanted to talk to Hiroko, and I thought about it each day, sulking in the heat of the Tanakas' luxurious guest bedroom. Earlier that afternoon the Tanakas had taken me to a local Buddhist temple to get me a blessing and there had been a skirmish. Takeyoshi had complained to me all the way to the temple about inscrutable American politics and then, inside the temple, had mysteriously pinched Fumiko, who stood beside me in the yellow-carpeted hallway. Fumiko exploded into tears and began kicking Takeyoshi's shins. He yelled at her, chasing her around the grounds of the temple and trying to pull her hair. Mr. Tanaka intervened, laughing, by hiding Fumiko behind him and nervously scolding his son. I stood and examined the shrine decorations, embarrassed for them, and tried to find something else to pay attention to.

When I reached Hiroko on the phone she seemed surprised to hear from me. "Hello?" she kept saying. "Where is Fumiko?"

"Fumiko is out," I replied. "Are you well?"

"You need help?" she managed to say. "You need Fumiko?"

"No," I said. "I just wanted to talk. How are you?"

"Hello?" she said again. After a few seconds, she seemed to understand I had called for her, but still tried to convince me to find Fumiko, that Fumiko was my friend to help me now. I gritted my teeth and agreed. Yes, I said. I'm with Fumiko. I like Fumiko. I'm fine. I thought about Hiroko and Junko playing jokes on each other and me, teasing each other after dinner. I thought about Junko crying at the train station. I wondered suddenly if I'd misunderstood this. Maybe Hiroko felt burdened by me? I tried to reconstruct our weeks together in my mind, to analyze every facial movement, each conversation. Hiroko's face wavered before me, her mouth twisted into a smirk. Feeling guilty, I excused myself and hung up. I calculated the time in America and called my parents.

"Are you having a wonderful trip?" my mother asked when I reached her.

"Sort of," I replied.

My mother sighed.

"You sound like Po Po," she said.

"What does that mean?"

"It means you should be grateful. Americans get to travel all over the world. It's a privilege."

"I don't think the Japanese see it that way. I think they see it as an invasion."

"Well, remember you've got something in common with them, at least. You aren't just like any other American."

"I'm exactly like every other American, Mom. Do you want me not to be an American?"

"Well, obviously you can't do that. I just expect you to appreciate what you're seeing. Be nice," she warned.

"What does that mean?" I asked again.

Over the line I could hear my mother chewing something. "What do you think?" she said, her mouth sticky with food.

We went on in this way until we began to argue about something in earnest, then tacitly agreed it was better to stop talking altogether. "Must clean," my mother hummed, digging into her bag of snacks. "Po Po and your uncle are coming over for dinner." I pictured my mother at the table with her brother and mother, telling them all about my phone call. *Oh, she's going through a difficult time. She doesn't understand and can't appreciate what she's seeing. She has no idea where she is.* Across from her Po Po passed plates of food to her daughter and favorite son, listening to the two of them talk, quietly, about their children.

The director thought we should have another banquet, so he invited all the scholarship students to a restaurant in Kobe near the Colony Yacht Club, a British expatriate meeting hall that was throwing its own Bon Odori festival. "Wear your yukatas," the director insisted. "You must come Japanese-style."

Fumiko seemed relieved that other host families would be there. "You will see Americans," she said, as if I'd been longing for them. In fact, I had been. "I will see Chizuko," she added dreamily.

The Colony Yacht Club was filled with British and Australian couples in sherbet-colored linen clothes, middle-aged men with their wives and teenage sons. They stood on the edges of a long, walled-in dirt courtyard that had faint lines for tennis or volleyball courts still chalked in with white, like dissolving vapor trails. Strings of lightbulbs dangled along the fences. The women appeared tall and red-faced in the glare. They stood in groups together clutching drink glasses beaded with perspiration in their left hands and conversed quietly, their mouths turned down and their eyes flickering to the face of each new stranger.

In the courtyard older Japanese women and men in costume danced in a circle around the usual wooden platform, or supervised games for children along the sidelines. The children at these games were also Japanese, clad in colorful yukatas or hapi coats, and they paid almost no attention to the white attendees at the celebration.

"Should we do something?" one of the Canadians asked. We had arrived quietly as a group, were acknowledged by the director and the president of the Colony Club, then ignored. "None of the club members seems to want to talk to us," he said.

We looked around. It was true. Heads snapped quickly away if we stared too long in strangers' directions. We milled and sulked. But, like particles attracted by an electric charge, eventually we broke up into groups based on nationality. We gathered in small circles, speaking so rapidly in our native tongues we sounded like we were hyperventilating. Fumiko and Mr. Tanaka eyed me from their position with the other Japanese host families and began walking over. I scurried from my group of Americans into the dance line.

I danced for several minutes behind a very enthusiastic older Japanese man in a black and white yukata who kept turning and grinning at me, showing off new dance steps. I smiled back and imitated him and the two of us bounced around the circle. At this, a Japanese reporter who had been invited to watch the festivities perked up. He was a short man with an enormous black camera dangling like a monkey from his neck. He watched me for a little while, then walked over and clamped his hand on my forearm to drag me out of the line. At first I didn't know what he wanted and so I panicked when his grip tightened. I walked back toward the circle, but he wouldn't let me go. His fingers dug into my arm, hurting me, making me recall the time I had been in a Kobe hotel exercise room, alone, when a Japanese man had come up and decided I was using the machinery the wrong way. He had grabbed my legs and tried to reposition me as I struggled. When I tried to get out of his grip, he reached out and slapped my bare thigh.

The dancers curved past in their circle. I tried to follow them, but the photographer pulled me roughly back toward him again. No one watched us. He began positioning my arms as if I were a doll, trying to make me dance the way I had danced in line. He hissed under his breath at me. Finally I acquiesced and made the motions. After one picture I started to walk away again, but he followed, dragging me out. Back and forth we fought, growling and grunting fragments of each other's languages.

Large droplets of the photographer's sweat fell onto my arm. I could feel his thigh on my thigh. He made a sound, or I did, like a snarling dog. "What?" I hissed. "What more do you want?"

Nonplussed, the photographer finally moved on to photograph the other dancers and I walked to the sidelines to calm down.

"I saw you dancing," said an older Englishman when I got there. He was fat and broad-shouldered, and his blond hair stuck in dark wisps to his forehead. He raised his glass and drank, looking me up and down.

"Did you see that photographer mauling me?" I replied angrily.

"Could you blame him?" he replied, smiling at my costume. "They told us to wear this."

The Englishman shrugged and looked off into the distance. A loudspeaker on the platform continued to thrum with women's high voices, the syllables trilling over us. "You managed to learn the dances," he said. "I've lived here five years and I couldn't do a step if my life depended on it. No grace, I suppose. No interest, really. But you've really gone native. You know, you even have the round face. The more I look at you, the more you look Japanese."

"I have to find a drink," I replied. I wandered around the yard, trying to avoid the Tanakas and the photographer, trying to find someplace I could be comfortable. Dancers snaked to the thudding drumbeat, listless, like the pulse of a headache.

"Some man," I said when I finally found my group of Americans, "just accused me of going native."

"Did he mean the yukata?"

"He meant my face," I said. "He said I looked Japanese."

"Well, isn't your mother Oriental?" one of the Americans asked. "I always thought—"

"No," I said sharply. "No. She's American."

"Of course she's American," the American replied sarcastically, but I interrupted again.

"I mean," I continued, "that she's white. We're white. We're completely American."

"Well, of course you are," he answered. He looked at me quizzically, glanced away while I fanned myself with a Colony Yacht Club pamphlet. I didn't want to say anything more, embarrassed about this lie and my insistence on its strange, misplaced patriotism. I sat on one of the few chairs left out for us instead and thought about my country across the ocean, what time it was there and how the mountains near my home looked in the purple evening. For a moment, I felt as if I owned it again, but then just as

49

quickly that feeling left. Dancers swept past the indifferent Yacht Club members. I didn't want the American beside me to respond to what I'd said, but he didn't know or care about what I'd admitted and so, because I had nowhere else to go and no one else to talk to, I sat with him in silence, watching the rest of the dance.

My parting gift from the Tanakas was an ikebana lesson. "You like Japanese tradition," Mr. Tanaka said. "You must learn ikebana." Fumiko frowned behind him. She had wanted to take me to the amusement park Hiroko and Junko had already escorted me to: a cross between Disneyland and an American 1950s diner. Everywhere we went, boys wore white T-shirts with their cuffs rolled up around cigarette or gum packages, their hair slicked back with pomade. Little American and British flags could be bought in carts set up around the square. Girls ate squid while wearing saddle shoes and strangely bell-shaped skirts. The day we went to the park, I remembered Junko insisted we end our time riding gigantic stuffed koala bears that were wired to lumber around the parking lot.

"Fumiko," Mr. Tanaka said, "will take you to your ikebana lesson. You will leave Japan appreciating Japanese style."

Fumiko walked me to the bus stop in silence. I could tell she was annoyed and so I thanked her for showing me around Kobe.

"I had a great time," I told her. "You've been so patient and kind."

She nodded. Her black bangs swung into her eyes, which she had circled with liner. Her lips were full and bright with lipstick. "I have been to Australia," she told me.

"Oh," I replied.

"I gained ten pounds from the food, it was very cheap. I loved Australia. There was so much space, so many animals."

"You should come to America," I told her.

She looked at me. "I have college and a job. I don't want to go to America," she said.

"I meant for a visit."

"I understand," she replied.

At the ikebana teacher's house, Fumiko sat on a nearby bench and worked on a lesson her teacher had given her the week before. She changed and rechanged the position of the flowers, trying to match the design her teacher had given her, perfectly.

The ikebana teacher gave me pink and green rice cakes to eat, then sat me by her side. She spoke to me in quiet Japanese, holding my hands in her own and moving them for me because I could not understand what she was saying. My hands followed her moves but I disliked the end result: one sparse iris drooped loosely to the far right, another was thrust straight into the center of the arrangement, like a cocked gun. The flowers annoyed me, they looked ugly and wrong. I yanked the irises off their positioning spikes and tried to screw them into new places, closer, farther away, different directions. The teacher laughed and chided me.

"No," she kept saying. "No."

She placed her hands over my own again and began to move them. The flowers smelled like fresh rain at the petals, like grimy metal and sweat at their stems. I tried not to jerk my fingers from under the teachers' hands, not to scratch at the delicate wrists held up before me. Fumiko watched as I wrestled as gently as I could from the teacher's grasp.

I like this! I said brightly over my wilting irises, the stem of one so bruised the flower head seemingly melted off its stalk.

The teacher chuckled more deeply. *No,* she said. *It's pretty this way, this way, don't you see?*

I glanced at Fumiko's perfect arrangement, its stiff and exactly matched complexity.

Don't you see? the teacher asked again. *Don't you see why this is more beautiful than that?*

I stared at Fumiko's arrangement. *It's easy,* I told myself. But still I couldn't do it.

No, I told the teacher, wiping my cheeks. *No.*

Sexy Mild

There is a Korean phrase, *hobak see gganda*, meaning a person who puts on the appearance of being modest or innocent, when in fact she is either dissipated or a sexual adventurer. It's not a phrase one says to the face of a person suspected to be *hobak see gganda* — the implications of the term are too insulting to be carried off lightly with anyone other than a close friend. It is a term that can apply to both sexes but is used most for women since, as the Koreans explained it, women lie more to protect themselves. I learned this over dinner with some Koreans who wanted to swap idioms with me; what did I mean by "two-faced," exactly? After I explained, one man leaned over to me, tugging the shirt sleeve of his wife. "*Hobak see gganda*," he joked. "She smokes, but not in public." Then he made blowing motions with his lips, his fingers dangling an invisible cigarette between them.

It is my fourth month of teaching as a Fulbright English teaching assistant at Usok Girls' High School, a private school located on the northernmost edges of a small, conservative town called Chonju in South Korea. My students like to ask me personal questions in class, such as whether I will sleep in the same bed with my American boyfriend, Joseph, when we travel, whether I French-kiss. Sex American-style is their obsession, which I have tried to overcome by wearing increasingly shapeless outfits to school, much to my appearance-conscious colleagues' dismay.

My students' scrutiny about my sex life worries me especially this week because I am giving a class lecture entitled "American Advertising." For visuals I brought magazine ads I'd selected in America months before, including one condom ad and an HIV public service announcement. Preparing my lecture, I perused their garish colors: the condom disk bright as any halo, the dance club shot of two men stippled with candy-colored lights as they danced face-to-face. I crumpled both up and tossed them.

My first class is unimpressed by the examples that I have saved, however. No stir over the tattooed Asian woman in the Gap ad or the black man with dreadlocks kissing the cheek of an Indian girl. My students flip the pictures over, hoping to find something more interesting. One of them discovers a picture of Claudia Schiffer in a Victoria's Secret bra and panties set (one girl asks if she can have it to pin on her wall) and holds it up for the class. They brighten. I point to a picture of Kate Moss sullenly glaring over a pair of CK jeans. I tell them that she used to be Johnny Depp's girlfriend.

"Oh, beautiful!" one stumpy girl from the back cries. I can't tell if she's talking about the model or Johnny Depp. When the conversation begins to die, I press them. "Is she dressed well?" I ask. "Does she have nice hair?"

The students mutter glumly to themselves, distressed at having to answer in English. "She's pretty because she looks cute. Not sexy," someone finally says. She holds up a picture of Cindy Craw-ford plucked from *Vogue*. Large-breasted, with smoky eyes and a lush red mouth, Cindy looks meaty compared to Kate Moss. Her small muscles ripple, her white teeth shine fiercely through parted lips. "You don't want to look like this?" I ask, and my entire class of fifty students, in unison, yells a disapproving "Noooo!"

I know my girls consider sexiness a compliment, however. They tease each other and me with the term in class, on the schoolyard, at lunch. Whether they dislike these American models because they find the women racially unattractive (some students have told me they think white women are hideous), they won't say. I press and press. Finally a student points out that the difference between liking what she sees and wanting to be what she sees is the value she places on sexiness in general. *Being sexy*, she explains in Korean, *only wins you the admiration of men while all the women hate you.*

According to my students, the Korean feminine ideal is quiet and cute, obedient (though this quality is loudly jeered at by many girls when listed), practical, smart. It is the image of Korean women I'd had myself before coming here. In America, I had envisioned Korean girls in floor-length skirts with heads bowed and eyes downcast, clad in dumpy black and blue uniforms. In Seoul, however, Korean women passed me on the streets in tight shorts that barely skimmed the line demarcating thigh from ass, clad in high-cropped tops and open-toed heels. Behind them rose the startling line of Seoul's buildings, skyscrapers looming in neon and shimmering steel, glass genies emerging through steam bursts from grates above the subway.

"Why do Americans like sexy?" a student asks.

"Because foreigners like sex," another student whispers.

"Do they really?" I ask.

"American women like sex," the student clarifies.

Blushing, I try to change the subject. "Where will you go for your winter vacation?" I ask the class. A mistake. They must attend school during winter break. The students groan at the question.

"American women like sex!" the student cries once more.

I give in. "Because some women may have sex before marriage?" I ask reluctantly.

"Yes," they chorus.

"Koreans *never* have sex before marriage?" I ask. I have just read in the English-language newspaper that 30 percent of all abortions in Korea are performed on teenagers. My students nod.

"Why do American women have sex without marriage?" the student demands.

"Some women," I begin, caught, "will have sex before marriage because they love their boyfriends."

"But you do not marry."

"Not always. If they don't get along . . . sexually, they may not marry. Sex is a kind of"—and here I blunder completely—"test," I say.

My students can't stop laughing.

In the *kyomushil* on break I swap makeup secrets and recipes with my female coteachers. I suspect they discuss more personal things when I am not around but, if they do, they don't feel comfortable speaking about them with me. I don't actually have makeup secrets, but I am beginning to invent them so that I don't continue to sit alone as I have for the past weeks. Fewer and fewer of my female colleagues are speaking to me. This is on account of my winter vacation, my plan to travel to the Philippines.

Today the cooking teacher tells me my outfit is pretty; she likes the way I've done my hair in its little "flip." She is one of the few women left who still make an effort to converse with me, so I smile and thank her. I don't mention that the "flip" is accidental because I don't have a hair dryer; the style is the result of my sleeping wrong.

You have a large nose, she adds, smiling but serious. She has been watching me leaf though old class lessons. She reads through them with me, pointing to the word "big" on my "Descriptions" word chart. She wants to learn English and practices on me; now she translates her phrase into English. "You have a . . . big nose," she says haltingly. *Americans have big noses,* she explains in Korean. Though our noses are almost the exact same size and shape, the cooking teacher, giggling, continues to insist on the difference.

Now she smiles again and opens her dictionary. According to my chart, the cooking teacher is tall and has short black hair with purple highlights. She has lined her full lips with a dark brown pencil, which shows through the brown lipstick she also wears. "Tomboy," she points to me, using my nickname. The actual but slightly less complimentary variation on this really translates to "hermaphrodite," but I don't tell her the English for it. The name was given me by my tae kwan do master after I beat a twenty-year-old male opponent in an impromptu sparring match. I'd backed the young man into a corner from the first round, terrifying him mostly with my foreignness and femaleness, the fact that I seemed aggressive.

The cooking teacher doesn't understand why I study tae kwan do for exercise, and seemed horrified by my sparring story when I told her. Nor does she understand why I don't wear makeup or high heels to school, why I want to travel so far from home alone to live in Korea, and why I now want to go to another foreign country during the school's winter break when I should teach. Although technically there are no classes scheduled, all the teachers and students must stay at school to cram for the college entrance exams. No mention of this was made in my Fulbright contract or by the principal upon my arrival, and now I feel frustrated and embarrassed by finding out this information too late to cancel my tickets. It puts the burden of my work unfairly on the other teachers, most of them women, and makes me look like how I feel: a twenty-five-year-old foreign heel.

"Do you take vacation?" the cooking teacher asks in English now, touching the lapels of her shiny brown suit. I flush, thinking about my undeserved trip, and she glances surreptitiously toward Mrs. Ko's desk.

Mrs. Ko, an English teacher, had been helping me negotiate with the principal about my vacation schedule. But now she isn't speaking to me. At lunch a week ago I overheard her and some other teachers shouting angrily in Korean at one another about the workload; Mrs. Ko complained about having to go home and take care of her children after so many hours at school. *I would love to go on vacation, too!* Mrs. Ko had snapped. She opened and slammed desk drawers, dropped papers. *I would like to travel!* she shouted.

I bowed my head as teachers shot looks in my direction. At the sound of the third class bell, Mrs. Ko swept past me with her class books, knocking over her mug of black tea as she rushed out of the room.

My new batch of students responds in exactly the same ways to the same advertisements as the last class. They cheer for the fey Kate Moss, comically revile Cindy Crawford on her red divan. Another student asks for the Victoria's Secret ad to take home. The only difference from first period is that these girls comment positively on my hair "flip" when I enter the classroom, making me wonder if the cooking teacher coached them to say this.

On break afterward, I go down to the school's lobby to call the Fulbright office in Seoul about my contract dispute. I am soon told angrily by the secretary that the problem is entirely my own. "We cannot handle every problem," Ms. Kim warns me. "You are the one responsible for this."

"But if they don't believe my contract is valid in the first place, how can they believe me?"

Ms. Kim coughs. She gets too many of these calls. "Compromise," she advises.

"I would, gladly, but I've already bought my plane tickets. They're nonrefundable. My school only told me they wanted me to stay two weeks ago!"

"Perhaps," she says, "you can pretend to be more gracious."

In the background I can hear phones ringing, the clatter of what sounds like a thousand typewriters.

"I feel terrible about this, but that doesn't change my ticket dates," I tell her.

"Your coteachers must work much harder than you and longer to accommodate you," she replies. "They don't tell you this, but it is understood. You must decide if your relationships here are more important than traveling."

"I understand this, but your office created this contract; *you* stipulated from the beginning that we get these weeks off!"

"And you are the one who must enforce it," she finishes. "This is your school. It is your decision." She pauses but I don't answer. I am trying to remember if someone at Usok ever took me aside to explain clearly what was expected of me. Had I misunderstood what the teachers had been telling me all this time? Some subtle reminder of what I should be doing? "If you have no more questions, I must go," she says.

After she hangs up, I stand staring at my distorted reflection in the school's silver pay phone. From down the hall, girls scream with laughter on their break. They run into the hallway with their brooms and mops to begin their daily cleaning hour. I watch as one of the class captains directs them with her back toward me, arms waving in her black jacket.

When she turns around, she looks disconcerted to find me slumped against the pay phone. "Oh! Sonsangnim," she cries, addressing me as "teacher." She wolf-whistles at my knee-length black knit dress, a surprising change from my usual pants. As she does this, three of my female coteachers walk by. They nod, eyeing the students. But when they hear the captain's appreciative whistle they slow down. They stare at me while they start to bow, their jaws working and working.

When I first arrived at Usok, the male Korean teachers came to my desk, individually, to ask questions. The history teacher struggled through Christian philosophy texts in English; he repeatedly wanted to know what the word "ekphrastic" meant and never believed me when I told him I couldn't find it in my dictionary. Mr. Chang, an English teacher, wanted to know if American women were more practical than Korean women. He is a shaggy-headed, middle-aged man with a hyena laugh who draws English-language cartoons in his spare time. "He is odd," Mrs. Ko whispered when I first met him, "but he may be a genius." Mr. Chang scratched his head furiously as he watched.

"I have observed," he said, "that you do not cry. American women do not cry. So, American women are more practical than Korean women. They are like Korean men."

"I don't know about that," I replied.

"Oh, yes," he said. "It is true. My wife is insane." Then he burst into huge, gulping laughs.

The question most male teachers asked, however, was whether I liked volleyball. I responded enthusiastically, Yes, I loved volleyball. Were the teachers going to play? They nodded. Every year, they told me, an afternoon tournament was held. There would be food and drink. It was imperative that I show up.

I went down to the volleyball courts the afternoon of the tournament and saw two teams composed of half the male faculty playing. A table of snacks was being prepared by members of the female faculty. I sat on the bleachers next to Mrs. Ko and the principal, a tall, heavyset man with balloon cheeks, and watched.

"Is this the first team?" I asked her.

"Yes, this is the first team."

"Who else is playing?"

Mrs. Ko pointed to a group of other male teachers gathered below us on the bleachers. They each wore white shorts and saggy cotton shirts. "They will," she replied.

"What about the women?"

"No," Mrs. Ko said. "Women do not play." She went back to inspecting the game, cheering when the principal cheered.

I looked at the women setting up the platters of squid and glistening dark grapes, the bowls of pale peanuts. They stood close together. I bowed to my principal and walked over to them. When I arrived, however, the women stopped talking.

"Rekdal Sonsangnim!" they cried.

Can I give you some help? I asked in Korean. Oh, no. The women shook their heads. No, you are a guest. You do nothing. They went back to dumping ice in a tin bucket, thrusting bottles of beer into its snowy mound like glass flags. I watched the game for a while and fumed, believing the question I had been asked about volleyball had been deliberately misleading; the male teachers had simply wanted me to come and serve them. And now I couldn't even do that. The cooking teacher offered me beige strips of dried cuttlefish, and I felt embarrassed at the sight of her thin hands, politely serving me. I tried opening packets of snacks but the women shook their heads and waved me away.

"There is no reason for me to be here?" I asked Mrs. Ko as she walked toward the table.

"Yes, there is no reason for you to be here," she replied. She blinked at me behind her black-framed glasses and went to stand with the other women who had positioned themselves behind the table, away from the volleyball court and me. I tried to find something to do with my hands and ended up wringing my fingers in my lap.

This is so boring, I heard one of the women hiss. Someone else whispered something I couldn't translate then and the women cackled behind their cupped hands. The principal strolled toward us. Talking stopped and beer was offered to him in a small glass. He beckoned me over. *Are you interested?* he asked me. *Yes,* I replied. He beamed at my answer and stretched to his full height. The women teachers took that as a cue to hurry over then and offer us both a bowl of grapes to eat. They smiled at me as I slipped a black grape in my mouth.

"You don't have any pure love in America," Mr. Chang says at my weekly two-thirty workshop. We are speaking about my American advertising lecture. It is after lunch and six teachers sit dozing in the science room, waiting for me to be finished. Frankly, I am waiting for me to be finished. At the beginning of the year I was told by our principal that the English faculty needed to meet once a week to converse with a native speaker and, being that native speaker, I was naturally volunteered. Outside of questions about American holidays and my personal history, however, no one says much. Lee Won Hee, my homestay father, plays with a pen on his desk. Mrs. Ko glares at the clock above my head.

"There is no virginity in your country," Mr. Chang explains. I look at him. The other teachers shift in their seats and perk up.

"We have a lot of people in America," I say, trying not to laugh. "Among them are some virgins."

Mr. Chang grins as he watches me.

I go back to feeling uneasy. How honest do they really want me to be? I wonder, though the question is pointless. I don't feel comfortable being honest about this topic, not with my colleagues. But the stranger or more irritating I am to them, the more oddly sexual I become; speculation about my sex life seems to be proportionate to how much information about me my coteachers can unearth. This is especially true about my travel and education history. For instance, after he discovered I went to graduate school in Canada, Mr. Lee asked if he could see me in a bikini. "I want to see your bikini," he whispered.

"Sharon Stone is my example," Mr. Chang continues. "She is not pure. And she is on TV to sell gas and the movies." He goes on to include various Caucasian women on Korean television advertisements, girls draped over couches moaning about chocolate and lingerie, pouting into the camera.

"They could be anyone," I tell him. "They're not necessarily American."

"Sharon Stone is American."

"Sharon Stone is not *all* American women," I argue.

"She is not Meg Ryan," Mrs. Ko adds indignantly. "Meg Ryan is special."

"Do you prefer Sharon Stone or Meg Ryan?" Mr. Lee asks me. The answer is simple: Only Meg Ryan is adored by Koreans. Only

Meg Ryan appears on Korean television dressed, improbably, as a nun selling a shampoo and skin cream called Sexy Mild. Even the label resounds with Meg Ryan's image: cute, perky, occasionally desirable. My students buy posters of her that swing from gift shop awnings, card-size head shots available in any music store. She is beautiful and girlish; the foreign equivalent of all the tiny Korean women giggling over children's toys and snack foods on television. There is something domestic about her as well as exotic; her adorable Americanness my students can comprehend because it is always bounded by something *they* want: a boyfriend, a happy family, true love.

"I don't really like either actress," I say, considering my options.

"That is because you are a hermaphrodite," Mr. Chang replies.

"Tomboy," I tell him.

"If Meg Ryan were here, she would marry me!" the normally quiet Mr. Kim explodes from the back of the classroom. He waves his arms and smiles at us. "Because I am charming!"

All the teachers laugh except Mrs. Ko, who adores Meg Ryan. She turns and glares at him. "You are insane," she says, pretending to tease him back.

"Meg Ryan is *hobak see gganda*; that is why Korean women like her," Mr. Kim continues to joke.

Mrs. Ko shakes her head fiercely, openly enraged now at the thought of her icon accused of being a dissembler. "No," she says. "No, you are wrong!"

"My wife likes Meg Ryan," Mr. Lee adds quietly. "I prefer Sharon Stone."

"I think we need to focus," I say, but it is too late. The teachers argue furiously about the merits of each actress, and I don't interrupt because they are at least arguing in English. I sit down and watch the clock. My job is done here. But then I think of what Mr.

Lee said, and then I think about Mr. Lee's wife, my homestay mother. I recall a conversation alone with her when Mr. Lee had slipped off to meet his male colleagues. Out came the little glasses of bad Korean wine she rarely sipped, a cigarette smuggled out late on the balcony. She had stared through her cigarette smoke at the tree-covered hill looming before our apartment building. *Do American women work and then clean at home?* she asked. A television show blared in the living room. We were standing by the daily laundry she had just hung to dry by hand, waiting to fold them up and iron them on the flat pastel board stored beneath the sink.

Yes, I replied.

Her eyebrow raised. *As many hours? And what do the men do?*

I told her a little lie. *The same as the women.*

She smiled. *I think you should tell Mr. Lee this when he comes home.*

"I think Rekdal Sonsangnim would be Sharon Stone," says Mr. Chang now, tapping his desk with a pencil.

"No, she would be Meg Ryan."

"She would be a man. She doesn't cry."

"You know," I interrupt. "None of this is different from America—"

"Excuse me!" Mr. Chang cries politely. "We are very different! Only you have Sharon Stone."

"I thought your point was that *everyone* had Sharon Stone," I say, but no one understands this.

The bell for fifth period rings then and the teachers file out, happy for once, because the conversation was simple to follow and interesting. In the hall my students smile and bow at me, but as always, they do not come forward. The first few months I assumed this was due to their nervousness about which language to speak with me—Korean? English? But now I suspect that it goes deeper than language, that it nestles at the core of what they believe I am.

And what do they believe I am? Another American woman who comes in with the slick and ordinary Western visuals, the same pop songs, the same bad Hollywood movies. No matter how much my Korean students ask about what my life in America is really like, I dissemble, I obfuscate the complex truth and show them Cindy Crawford, Victoria's Secret, Kate Moss. Perhaps my students believe this is all I really want.

Or perhaps, I realize, seeing students cringe in surprise at the sight of me by the washroom sink, I am someone who doesn't appear to want anything, who wanders and wanders. Lacking the specific desires of a woman they understand, there are no limits to what I may say or do or think, and the more I tell my students about my life and America—however little that may be—the more it seems I am trying to convince them that my life is as available to them as to myself. And they are frightened by this selfishness, this boundaryless existence.

It strikes me now that I do not want to teach my students anything like this. I don't want them to become too adventurous or sexually liberated, living lives that may be painfully isolating in a town like Chonju. I don't want my students to have to suffer recriminating looks and remarks; I want them to be happy. Now I'm in the odd position of thinking that this happiness might be best achieved by their being conformists, and dislike the impact I can see my advertising visuals and daily presence make on some of my more impressionable students. The truth is that after several months here I have begun to envy my students and coteachers who know what it is they should want and know how they must behave. Yes, I reject these things—cuteness, early marriage, an appearance of docility—just as I have rejected them in America.

But in America I see that I had the luxury to reject them, being fluent in the language and cultural dynamics to find people similar to myself. Here I do not know what to say or whom to talk to; I am and am not familiar with the rules for being an acceptable young woman. And while I can see how such an insular community as Chonju can condemn people, especially women, to living narrower lives, I can also see how this community protects those absorbed into its order. After living so many months in Korea, I want some of that protection. I want to know I am doing the right thing—whatever that means here—and be the good girl who knows her place and responsibilities. Intellectually, I know this is bad for me, this is potentially bad for my students, but I can't help but feel it. I am lonely, and I want this loneliness taken away.

You should wear this, I remember my homestay mother told me one evening, pulling out a wisp of a dress. I laughed.

Maybe in Seoul, I told her.

She looked disappointed putting the dress back in my closet.

You know, Teacher Lee told me he wants to travel during summer vacation, I said.

She smiled as if that were unlikely.

Won't you go, too?

She considered this a while. *I've never been out of the country*, she said.

Never? Where did you go on your honeymoon?

She glanced at her hands and pointed out the window. *Seoul*, she replied. And jabbed her cigarette north, showering red sparks across the balcony parquet.

At four o'clock I go with Mrs. Ko down to the principal's room. Entering the long room, carpeted with tatami and decorated with paintings of Chinese calligraphy, I take off my shoes and shuffle into the plaid slippers Mrs. Ko offers me. I pad after her to the low coffee table ringed with brown, overstuffed leatherette couches shaped like gigantic mushrooms. A tank of red and gold carp shimmers in one sunny corner, lucky fish, lucky omens.

My rudimentary Korean unnerves Mrs. Ko, who tells me it is better for someone to translate for me rather than to try the patience of the principal, who is a busy man referred to behind his back as "the Dictator." I feel guilty having Mrs. Ko, who still dislikes me, translate my negotiations. But Mrs. Ko volunteered to help and continues to volunteer. Unlike other teachers, she says, she will not ignore her duty. She sits on the opposite corner of the couch that we share now, her legs pressed together tightly.

The principal enters the room and greets us both. He sits and offers me tea which Mrs. Ko, glancing pointedly at me, convinces me not to accept. A busy man. He starts talking.

"He says he knows you will leave Korea," Mrs. Ko repeats in English. "He says he needs you to teach winter classes. This is your duty to our students. You must stay."

"Tell him that I want to stay," I say to Mrs. Ko. "I want to stay and teach because I love our students. But I didn't know about the winter classes before I bought my plane tickets. If I had, I would have remained. The Fulbright office gave us our contracts; I followed the Fulbright contract."

"The Fulbright contract is not complete," Mrs. Ko translates, and I know that this is both a lie and the truth. The principal signed the papers; he simply means that no written contract between us could possibly be complete. Work responsibility is socially decided upon and maintained in Korea. It is a matter of loyalty, not paper. "There was never any contract sent from the Fulbright office to us," she adds, lying again.

"Then please, call Ms. Kim at the office," I reply. "I'm sure she'd *love* to help you." A flurry of rapid Korean follows and I think of Ms. Kim, coughing disappointedly on the phone. I think of all the arguments and conversations about me burning through the phone wires, traveling across high-tension lines. Then I think of my female coteachers, eating together in small groups on the other side of the *kyomushil,* away from me at my desk.

"Tell him not to call her," I say, changing my mind. "Tell him I will stay to teach for vacation."

Mrs. Ko stops talking. "You will stay?" she asks.

From the corner of the room comes a bubble and splash from where a carp, chased by another carp, thrashes suddenly to the surface. "I'll give up the tickets," I say. "It's not worth it."

She translates this to the principal, who puffs out his cheeks and looks at me.

"Are you sure?" she asks for him.

I nod. The principal looks deeply confused as he considers this new option, surprised at my change of heart, and I wonder if he thinks this is merely a tactical move on my part. After a few moments he shakes his head knowingly, smiles, then begins speaking to Mrs. Ko.

"He says you must go," Mrs. Ko translates, looking confused herself. "You are an American teacher and this is not expected of you." The principal looks strained, red-faced. He purses his already protruding liver-colored lips and nods.

Where will you go? he asks me in Korean.

The Philippines.

Alone?

No, principal. I will travel with two female friends.

It is dangerous, he replies. *It is not as advanced as Korea. It is very dangerous.* He suddenly stops and looks around the room as if he should change his mind once more, but doesn't. *Be careful,* he tells me instead.

Mrs. Ko and I bow and prepare to leave as the bell rings for the final class of the day. The principal says something quietly in Korean to Mrs. Ko and she nods and hurries after me.

"He says," Mrs. Ko tells me as we step into the hall, "that it is fine for you to go because you are American and do not understand our responsibilities."

"This is true," I say. "I do not understand."

"Why do you want to stay?" she asks.

"To help you."

"But you cannot help us. You do not know what to do in class."

Now I am the one who is confused. "But you would have taught me, wouldn't you? You wanted me to stay."

"We did not expect you to. It is not like an American to do that. They have different lifestyles." Mrs. Ko smiles rustily at me. "Would you come over to my house one afternoon this week?" she asks. "My children are very eager to see you." I accept her invitation, even more confused now, and watch her walk down the stairs to her last class. Students swarm between us. I make my way to the teacher's sleeping room on the second floor to retrieve a book, but when I try to open the door with the old key I have been given, the door, as usual, sticks. I yank it as hard as I can, but the door will only slide enough to let me squeeze through. For a brief moment I am caught between the door and the jamb as the class bell rings, and I struggle there, violently.

Two weeks ago, when I began planning for my Christmas vacation abroad, I had visions of myself as brash and flirtatious, drinking a little too much at a bar perhaps, wearing a bikini on the beach, my face growing dark from the sun. The first thing I did was get my hair cut. Korean makeup. Then a slip dress. Putting on the dress at home, I felt as if I had stripped layers and layers of myself off, and indeed I had: there was the pile of colorless long dresses and pants I had over the months donned for school, now abandoned like the bulky exoskeleton of a spider. I sat on my bed and tried on the makeup, wiped it quickly off. I tried to wear the dress out—the same style hundreds of young Korean women wore—and found myself wrapping sweaters and scarves around me, masking my body. I ate out with my head or eyes down. I even took to covering my mouth with my hand when I laughed. I found myself unconsciously tugging my dark cardigan so that it covered more of my chest area, buttoning and unbuttoning it as strangers' questions became more personal.

It would be too easy to blame this on Korea. It would be a vast oversimplification to say that my behavior became more Korean as well, since few Korean women my age cover their mouths when they laugh or have qualms about wearing revealing clothing and dramatic makeup. I told myself that it was simply understanding the public difference between American femininity and Korean femininity that caused this behavior, but instead I felt as if a personality that had lain dormant a long time inside me had bloomed. This other me is not the adventurer, not the self-reliant or modern androgyne. She is timid and repressed, conflicted as to the value of her independence. She is also too deeply rooted in me to be any recent implant. I had a sudden, and nasty, suspicion that the independence of spirit I thought was inherent in me was most likely a veneer: the true me might really be the docile woman I'd been taught to be since birth, the girl even my students despised. If this was the case, my Korean coteachers have given me a pointed nickname with "Hermaphrodite." They can see what I don't want to: that my pretensions to any sort of masculine privilege here are merely for show. I am and possibly always have been protecting myself by pretending not really to be a woman, and certainly not an American one, loaded with all that monolith's crude expectations and dangers.

This is not something I can explain now, speaking with Mr. Chang. "Have you heard," he asks before darting down to the schoolyard to meet his waiting wife, "about the teenage girl who gave birth to a baby in a rest stop? She didn't know she was pregnant. She left the baby in a trash can." I bunch the neck of my sweater up tight in one fist. It is right before my last class of the day and I am exhausted, hoarse, irritable.

"American schools," I sigh, "have a lot of problems with sex education."

"Oh, no," he says, "it wasn't in America. It was in Seoul. The girl was Korean."

I look at him. "Oh," I say.

"Yes," he says, smiling. "This is a real problem in Korea. This isn't the first time it's happened."

Not knowing what to say, I shrug and mutter, "It's a problem everywhere," and leave. But in class I find myself watching the students closely as they pore over the advertisements. I have to swallow my sarcasm when another student repeats what I have heard throughout the day: *Korean girls never have sex before marriage. It is better to be cute than sexy. It is better not to stray too far.*

I look at my students who are busy laughing, clutching one another other for comfort when I speak to them directly. But I am tired and do not want to struggle through the story Mr. Chang just told me. Instead, I smile and ask if they suspect even a few girls are having sex before marriage. Maybe, I suggest, someplace like Seoul?

"Noooo!" comes the shout, and I sigh. But to my far right one of the better students raises her hand. "Maybe," she says. Her mouth works like she wants to say more, but she stops, embarrassed by her insufficient vocabulary. The other girls ignore her, already engrossed in the Victoria's Secret layout, and so I move on, nodding appreciatively at her honesty. It's five o'clock and I want to go home. There are limits to what can be shared, I know. There are limits to what everyone can say.

Other Women

The day my boyfriend comes to visit Usok in Korea we are trapped in the teacher's narrow cafeteria, eating while girls pound and pound on the black door.

"Sonsangnim!" one of them cries behind Joseph, whom I have positioned with his back to the glass. We hear a crash; the girl has fallen off the chair she's propped near the window to get a good look. Whoops erupt from the crowd outside and girls suddenly scatter, swallows wheeling over rice paddies in springtime.

"They've been waiting all year for this," I tell him.

He smiles and, after the girls have been warned to go to class, follows as I lead him through the grainy interior of the school's basement, past its sweetshop and drink dispensers. Joseph tried to mask his surprise upon first seeing the building, but I know how it appears. My students call this place in Korean "the madhouse on the hill" because it is set high on a little ridge that overlooks several acres of paddy and was used, years ago, as a war hospital. The school kept its institutional look: stark white on the outside, stripped bare of any decoration or furniture in the interior. The ceilings are gray to match the salt-and-pepper cement floors; the white walls have crosshatches of cracks running through the plaster. There is no insulation or heating to speak of, and so in the winter the school sets up what look like enormous timed Bunsen burners in the classrooms and *kyomushil*, around which everyone huddles, holding their hands before them with their fingers spread wide apart as if to catch a basketball. In the spring they fumigate the entire building by running a man-sized black tube through the main hall which they hook up to a pesticide truck, and let the chalky air billow and wreathe through the empty classrooms.

Joseph lags behind as I trot him past the senior girls' rooms. I can hear the scrape of chairs as students leap from their seats, press faces and fists to the window. "Sonsangnim!" they wail as we speed by.

Joseph opens his mouth to ask why we can't slow down, but I tell him to wait. Break is about to begin. As the buzzer screams and the doors fling open, I stand Joseph by the trophy case in the hallway and start directing traffic. "All right!" I yell to the girls as they rush toward us. "Don't kill him."

The girls laugh and swarm around him, whip cameras out from pockets and backpacks. "Please," they say in broken English. "One. Just. Picture." They are entranced by his blue eyes, his dark brown hair and large nose. Joseph smiles, the girls swoon. *Snap snap.* They push me close beside him, themselves closer. *Snap snap.* I get copies of these photos on my desk all next week, one by one, like dark little hints.

You can see me in our best one standing off to his left, Joseph's skin looking strangely alabaster in the flash. Clutched under his arm, I'm smiling tightly, trying not to show my teeth.

For months Joseph threatened to come see me in Korea, possibly move here from Michigan, where we met over a year and a half ago at a party. We've spent more time apart in our relationship than together, since I began dating Joseph just five months before I received a Fulbright to Korea. When I discovered I would be moving, I assumed that Joseph and I would break up, but, to my surpise, this has not happened. Instead we write letters and call each other. We make promises to visit. Joseph is the first man I have dated seriously since breaking up with Mark three years ago. Joseph himself is divorced; we both agreed that the other was the first person we had met whom we wanted to live with since our breakups. This does not mean, however, that I want him to live with me in Korea. "Don't you dare come here," I warned him over the phone.

"I won't," he replied. "I probably won't. Don't you miss me?"

"Of course," I said. "But all that would change if you moved here."

We planned elaborate and unlikely vacations together: Australia's Great Barrier Reef, Indonesia, Cambodia. Instead, I traveled around Korea alone or with friends, riding the massive green buses packed with women in white blouses and dark skirts, boys crammed three or four to a seat like crates of fruit. I sent him dutiful love letters from Chejudo and the DMZ. But though I longed for him certain nights in teahouses or at bars I occasionally patronized, I argued against his coming.

"I'm beginning to think you don't like me," he said.

"I'll risk it," I replied.

Finally he began to get irritated. "Is it that your school doesn't want visitors?" he asked petulantly one night. I was calling from a pay phone outside my apartment building. The night guard waved furiously at me to attract my attention; I had become the building superstar since moving in. Now he had to speak with me, the American, every time I left the protection of my apartment.

"The opposite," I told him. "Every day the teachers ask why we're not married."

"Tell them I'm already divorced," he said.

The guard gave up waving and sat back down in his little booth, watching me closely.

"I have a week off from work," Joseph continued. "Plus Easter. Why don't I come then?"

"Fine," I replied. "Just remember I can't be responsible for what will happen."

I could tell from Joseph's crooning murmur he thought I was referring to some great overflow of affection, but I wasn't. I was thinking about Diane. I had seen her again that morning, sitting at the back of the bus with her badly done lipstick, waving. Stout-bodied, with cropped, rusty hair, she has a complexion that runs the gamut between mottled and milky, which reminded me, in the window's harsh glare, how quickly white women age.

"You know that man, Tom?" Diane had asked me on the bus. She was referring to her off-again, on-again lover, Tom, whom she'd caught flirting with a young Korean woman. I watched her face contort, smooth, contort again. "What did you think of him?"

"I didn't get much of an impression," I said.

"Korean women sure like him."

"Has he ever dated one?"

"Occasionally. He shows up with one when he gets lonely. He's using them. And they use him for the prestige. Asian girls think it's cool to date white men."

"I guess you don't like it," I said, feeling suddenly uncomfortable.

"I'm surprised that he started dating one at all. Whenever I see them I feel so, well . . ." she let it trail off.

"Betrayed?" I asked.

"Yes," she replied.

"You can come," I told Joseph, "but don't get excited by what you find here."

He agreed and we hung up. I stood at the pay phone and gathered up my collection of plastic phone cards. Outside my booth a few teenage boys were making their way home late from the *hagwans*. The guard watched them as they approached me at the phone booth, stood hopefully to intervene, then sank back down again when he realized that I was safe. He waved and waved at me.

The company of foreigners in Korea is sporadic, difficult to find but distressingly easy to maintain. People feel things for one another here that they would never feel in the States. For instance: Chris is a half-Korean English teacher, living in Taegu for the year, who comes to visit me in Chonju occasionally and considers us "close." We are not friends. Deep down, we actually dislike each other. Still, the week before Joseph arrived from America, Chris invited himself over to wander the streets of Chonju, to provide me a kind of moral support, he said, for the future.

"This is what will happen," he said. "OK. He'll propose and you'll give in, but you won't really want to, but you'll feel you can't do any better so you'll move back to America and by that time he'll regret asking you, but he'll feel too bad to back out and you'll really start to regret accepting him, but it will be too late. You'll get married and the two of you will stay together forever, but both of you will secretly be miserable. Am I right? Am I right?"

"Don't you have any other friends?" I asked.

"Plenty of friends. Plenty of other friends," he said. "They're all women and they all hate me, but I have them."

We walked toward the shopping district where the five dilapidated movie houses lay nestled between restaurants and expensive clothing stores. The theaters are owned by the same family and each one has the same style of billboard painted in fluorescent orange and red paints with scenes from current movies. Beside these are tiny bakeries and restaurants, the windows patterned blue and black and white with their menus in Korean. Because there are so many stores and cafés on each floor of the shopping district buildings, neon signs appear to jut out from every edge and corner, looking as if they are stacked on top of one another. There are no sidewalks and none of the streets in the shopping district are wide; silver and blue taxis streak past shoppers, turn corners wildly, almost run over groups of teenage girls walking together arm in arm.

Chris grabbed my elbow for safety when a taxi swooped too close. Chris is tall and lanky, with thinning black hair and the kind of skin that looks sandpapered. But he's handsome, too, and so Korean women stared when he walked by. That Saturday, on the street together, we took in the Korean women's black lipstick and pancake foundations. They reminded me of a picture I once took of my female coteachers at school, the flash refracted off the silicates in their thick face powder. The result was a row of mortuary figures: pink necks, fishbelly faces, the eyes dully fixed. Chris stared back at the women and muttered about what it would be like to lick all that makeup off, layer after layer.

I jostled Chris on the street when he cast too many backward glances. "What?" he asked. "I'm single and all my female friends hate me and I can't even look?" I shrugged.

"Are you jealous?" he asked.

I shook my head. It was Chris, I knew, who was jealous, who got angry seeing the German manufacturer with his Chinese wife, the Englishman with the Korean prostitute. It was Chris who sneered as they walked down streets hand in hand or slightly apart, the women trailing behind. Whenever we ran into a mixed couple, Chris would trail behind them for blocks, foaming at the mouth.

"You're the jealous one," I said. "What do you find attractive about them?"

"Are you fucking blind?" he replied.

After our American movie, we walked back into the shopping district, strutted down alleyway after alleyway looking for food we both wanted to eat, bumping into people as we tried to find space in the crowd. And always, pasted on walls and billboards, the same blank Caucasian faces stared back at us: the blonde who looked as if she were twelve, hugging her knees violently to her chest, the brunette on a football length of nuclear-green turf with legs that appeared to entirely lack muscle. And the men. Tall and broad-shouldered and white, they lurked in advertisements behind their women like gangsters or knelt in supplication, their large eyes wide. By appearance at times angelic, at times as frightened as if they knew they'd been snapped up and whirled into another world entirely, these white men stared out at their audience as if to ask us how they ever got here. For a moment, looking at these men with Chris, I couldn't move in the crowds of Korean girls that seemed to surround us. Were they angry? Curious? Disgusted? I saw them staring at the advertisements: black-haired, black-eyed, their girlish faces as round as the camera lens snapping and snapping at their desires. I held my breath and pushed back into the crowd.

Today at school seeing Joseph, my students pressure me to set them up on meetings with American boys, alternating this demand with requests for Joseph's photograph. I cannot and do not comply with this largely because of the volume of these requests. Instead, I try to satisfy my students' curiosity about American dating habits with brief lectures in English. Their image of American high school is a combination of *Grease* and *Dangerous Minds*; my students go back and forth between quizzing me on what it was like to be prom queen (my school never had one) and whether I knew anyone who got shot.

Joseph, however, constitutes the bulk of their interest. At first, I suspect it is because they have no male coeds, but then I remember bringing in Chris for a disastrous show-and-tell session, how my students complained when they discovered he wasn't fully white. Their feeble interest dried up, exhausted itself. *My friend In-Suk said her American teacher brought in a white boy last week,* one of the third-year students complained in Korean. *When will you bring one in?*

Joseph, on the other hand, is fine: all-American. Tall and boyish, in person he appears to be that precise combination of bad boy and Romantic poet my girls worship from their Korean soap operas. Today he wears a white T-shirt and baggy khakis, clean brown shoes, a green rain jacket outside. His hair sparkles with blond highlights shot through his bangs. His crooked teeth gleam between lips chapped by the cold weather.

With Joseph at school, girls flood the halls, dash to the windows to throw down notes and candy, follow us (or, more accurately, him) as they beg to have their pictures taken beside us. At one point in the schoolyard my boyfriend is surrounded by upward of a hundred students. Their navy blue uniforms threaten to engulf him as the girls jostle and push to stand closer, making him look like the one white boat in a stormy black sea.

"Why are you so excited?" I ask in class.

"We never see men!" a girl shouts back.

"But you do," I argue, "all the time. Almost all the teachers here are men."

"They aren't American," a girl with butchly cropped hair calls out. "They aren't handsome!" another cries. Students ask if they can have my boyfriend's address. I imagine the thousands of love letters and photos he will be inundated with. "Give your letters to me," I say, hoping to curtail the certain deluge. "I'll give them to him." My students jeer at this display of possessiveness and dash away to the nearest store to buy him candy.

"Has an alien landed?" Mr. Chang jokes. I look at Joseph and try to see him as the Koreans see him. Now the brown hair appears eerily washed out, the large blue eyes comical, like those of a stuffed play toy. His slightly prominent nose I also think suddenly huge, his charming manners becoming sycophantic in my imagination. I hide him in the teachers' lounge as best I can and trot him out a little more sourly each class hour. We are pelted with personal questions about our first date, our possible engagement. My boyfriend sits on an overstuffed cushion on the highest chair in the room. He smiles and winks. My students swoon.

"Beatlemania from hell," I mutter as he hugs me to rapturous applause. They are already imagining our wedding: me in the sulfur-bright glare of the wedding photographer's gaze, a hail of rice like bits of soap sticking into the corners of my gown.

I peer into Joseph's face as he pulls me close. A series of bright angles, hard and unavailable features. *I don't look like that*, I think, searching for the one thing similar to myself. I find it in his eyes: the reflection of me swollen like a fun-house mirror image. I look deeper into them, myself blue on darker blue. *Snap snap.* I can almost hear the camera bulbs popping, drowning me out in the flash.

———

I love the fact that Joseph can't speak Korean. I love this fact with a vengeance, and speak more fluently with him beside me than I have for months, used to bumbling in line for train tickets or directions. I am already more than a bit of a snob about speaking Korean, since so many foreigners do not bother to learn it, can't read Hangul. After an eight-week intensive language program and a year's worth of living in a Korean household, I've become obsessed with speaking well. So Joseph sits patiently at the restaurants I select, a little bewildered as I rattle off his dish choices in terse, colorless descriptions that do not help him anticipate the meal that arrives. He has a low tolerance for spices. I order pork to barbecue and line fresh garlic on the grill for him to eat lightly charred, still pungent and raw on the inside. I feed him soondubu chigae, a peppery red soup laced with soft white tofu and baby clams, so hot it makes his nose run. I ask the waitress for more kojuchang, sprinkle the spicy pepper sauce liberally over his kalbi or bi bim bap.

I also like the fact that at the end of the meal I must pay because I am the one who can count in Korean. That is, until we find ourselves in a takkalbi restaurant and I see a young mixed couple our age, and watch the Korean woman order for the white man. I hustle Joseph out of the restaurant. On the way home I insist he memorize the Korean numbers one by one.

We stay at a *yogwan*, a cheap hotel, because my room at my homestay family's house is too small, too inappropriate. "It would be improper," I tell Joseph. "They think I'm a virgin." He laughs so hard one of the grape drinks I buy him comes up his nose.

"He is exactly what my wife expected he would look like," my homestay father tells me at dinner. "He looks like Brad Pitt." I tilt my head when I look at my boyfriend later and, maybe it's the angle, maybe it's the fact I have been surrounded by Koreans for a year, he does begin to resemble Brad Pitt, whom I despise. Alone in our hotel, I unroll the soft futon mattress on the slippery floor and watch Joseph take off his shirt, examining all the little muscles of his back under the fluorescent light. They make me feel ungrateful. "The great white shark," I tease Joseph when he bites my neck. But that night I dream I nourish a pearl: a hard, waxy little alabaster baby that rolls inside me like a marble.

"You don't find any of the Korean women specifically attractive here?" I ask the next day, and Joseph glances at me.

"I wouldn't be human if I didn't," he says.

But later he drops certain placating comments. "Too thin," he sniffs at the college girls wobbling by on their high black heels. "No muscle tone. Why do they cover their mouths when they laugh?"

"Good try," I tell him, and he looks hurt.

In bed at the *yogwan* he praises what is neutral on my body. "Beautiful kneecaps," he says, kissing them gently. "I love your shapely ears."

Another day in class. Students want to know if Joseph, like Brando, rides a motorcycle. They've seen the stationery with this image on it, the posters sold in card shops. I try not to cringe when one student tells Joseph that she prefers American men to Korean ones. My girls are young, and I don't believe they are attracted simply to my boyfriend's Caucasian features, but to the romanticism my students associate with them. When my students ask about Joseph, they want to know how he *feels* about me, what he *thinks* about me. What kind of wife he wants.

Joseph smiles wickedly when I finish translating this last question. But he is an earnest man who wants to preserve any illusion of equality between us that he can.

"Someone smart and independent," he answers seriously in English, and the girls who can understand cheer. We listen to the buzz of voices as his answer gets repeated over and over in Korean down the row of desks like a game of Secret. I cannot imagine what the girls at the end of each row must finally hear, but they beam even harder at Joseph when they do and squeal when he looks directly at them.

"I love you!" one girl calls out.

By our fifth show-and-tell class hour, I suspect that were Joseph much uglier or simply, like me, more common-looking—not the shocking blue eyes, not the height—they would still scream. My girls love him so hysterically because they imagine how he would love them back; they think they know how he would court them from the films they watch and the stationery sets they buy: the smooth, bland, intangible words of love that seem always to come in English spread in pink and yellow and black atop the creamy sheets, accompanied by ducklings and movie logos and romantic Japanese cartoons. "Darling so much I miss you" "My heart is a lit-bulb . . ." "My sweet friend when rain downs do you think on me?" The grammar is always wrong, the expressions awkward, as if the writers know passion can't be stated well or at all, thus must be printed in this other language to excuse it. Some sheets even come typed up in a truly barbarous Latin, suggesting desire's own arcane quality, its vocabulary a collection of dead syllables.

I've never seen romantic stationery in Korean. *There must be some*, I think to myself, and later paw through the notepads in my desk, the fresh packets sold at school supply shops. But the ones I can find are always in English, I see, or French or Latin. And suddenly it occurs to me that this is sad, but because these cards seem to be spoiling something about Korea. I dislike the oversentimental and unrealistic words in English for love, the American pressure to make fabulously romantic and public declarations about private commitments. I don't like the fact that, to me, these cards appear like lies imported from another culture, a cheap sentimentality that feeds off the educationally enforced separation of the sexes.

Though I have often accused Koreans of whitewashing the truth about themselves with ritualized politeness, with Joseph at Usok I suddenly do not find this much different from the romantic movies and singers America produces in huge volumes on a seemingly daily basis. I do not see this as being very different from myself and Joseph either, sitting in front of my students, pretending that we understand what loving each other means to each of us, what we expect from each other as months and years pass, what sacrifices we are prepared to make to stay together. Perhaps the two of us are simply putting on a show to please my students based upon what we think they want to hear about us: not Joseph's divorce, not the other men I may or may not have had sex with, and certainly *not* any hesitations I might have about dating Joseph because he's white. Perhaps my students, seeing movies from my culture, buying stationery in my language, have been taught to believe this artificial sentimentality is all that really matters to us. And maybe that makes them sad, too.

But there is nothing artificial about the expression Joseph wears in front of my class. It is genuine love, for me and for pleasing my students. He is telling them now how he saw me for the first time in Ann Arbor across a room—a crowded one of course—at a reading given by a popular author. He saw me, Joseph explains, and immediately he knew, he knew. . . . He trails off and looks at me. *What?* I look archly back. But now he's off, fleshing out what he knew about me from that first glance in such specific detail it is almost cruel to hear. No stray lock of hair is left undescribed. No simple gesture ignored. This part of his love is true, I understand, and I do not want to perceive this nakedness in him in front of them, our audience. But speaking about love to my students, Joseph gains a brilliance I have never seen before. It is one certainly few Korean boys their age possess, isolated among their own gender and kind. To my students it marks him as a true and native son from the Land of Hallmark, Cupid's Country: America, that nation of easy yet passionate commitment.

Joseph finishes. He turns to look at me. The room, for once, is silent; the Koreans digest what he said in greedy chunks. Even my poorest students seem to be getting it. Now suddenly they are on their feet, all of them, cheering and clapping and taking pictures. "Kiss!" they scream. "Kiss! Kiss!" And we do, and Joseph does, tipping me back so that my fingers nearly touch the floor. He brushes his lips over mine and sets me back on my feet to the furious snapping applause of cameras.

"Did you like that?" Joseph asks me, smiling. Behind him I can hear the girls chanting. "Jo-seph! Jo-seph! Jo-seph!"

"I don't think that matters," I reply, and try to look delighted when he again snakes his arm around my waist.

On our train to Seoul, I fiddle with Joseph's chair, hit the buttons with my fist, knocking it back into reclining position. I hit it again and send the foot rest scooting forward. Joseph grunts as his chair contorts and bucks him into a prone position. "Doesn't it make you sick?" I demand. "Doesn't it make you want to vomit?" I shove Joseph's arm roughly with each question.

"Why should it?" he says, but he isn't looking smug. "They don't know me; they're curious."

"This goes *way* beyond curiosity."

"They're high school girls."

"They worship you for no good reason!"

"You'd prefer they have a reason to worship me?"

I look out the train window to watch towns, mountains, golden fields shoot by. We are about to pass under a small stone bridge on which several little boys stand. They point excitedly to what looks like our car and wave and hoot and flash their middle fingers. *They must have seen us,* I think. Koreans don't give the bird to one another.

"Why does it upset you?"

"Why do you think?"

"I don't know; that's why I asked you." We look away from each other, huffy. The concessions man pushes his silver cart beside us, nodding to his Korean snacks in plastic wrappers. Joseph despises the smell of dried squid. I order a packet.

"Jesus," he says as I tear open the plastic.

"Too exotic for you?" I ask. I rip off a flattened tentacle and gnaw on it.

"Jesus," he says again. "Look, people seemed to like what I was saying so I went with it."

"Did you," I say, chewing furiously on the final suction cup, "realize when you saw me in the red sweater and the black leggings and my short hair, did you also see I was half Asian?"

Joseph looks at me. "No," he says. "Yes. No. I saw," he begins, "and I didn't."

"Well, you're going to have to think about what that means," I say. We sit back and feel the train rock beneath us. It has been three days since Joseph arrived. He leaves in another two. I try, and fail, to move my hand to cover his knee.

"Forgive me if I refuse to believe this is about me being a fetishist," Joseph announces without looking at me.

"I know you aren't a fetishist," I snort. "All your ex-girlfriends are blond."

All the muscles in Joseph's jaw jump. The Koreans who are staring at us already try even harder to understand what we are saying. I nudge him and take out a book to read. He leans back and pretends to sleep. Outside, beyond the green and brown fields, the solitary restaurants and battered houses, there are mountains, large and smoke-colored, covered with trees in white springtime blossom.

Are they married? the beautiful Korean woman across from us murmurs.

Probably, her husband replies, leaning back and closing his eyes. *They're fighting, aren't they?*

That night I have a nightmare in which Joseph marries an Asian woman. She is like all the college students and stewardesses and salesgirls I've seen in Korea: the perfectly swept-back hair reddened with dye, arms thin and pale as cigarettes, the symmetrical face certain attraction studies indicate are ideal. The eyes are, perhaps, cosmetically enhanced or surgically altered to resemble a white woman's. But there the similarity of appearance ends. In this dream she's mute because she can't speak English; still, she blossoms. She is the ideal for every woman. But the prevalence of her looks in Korea suggests she is really possible to achieve. She is, in fact, an attainable, if not genetically inherited, virtue. She smiles when Joseph speaks, sits by his side and always finds the romantic edge to disappointment, love's shortcomings. When Joseph sees her he can no longer fake attraction to me. I am just another example of how difficult it is to be with someone who thinks she understands exactly what you want in life, and inherently distrusts it. Here are all my failings and idiosyncracies now, spilled out on the table like so many bad groceries.

When I wake I feel guilty. *Somehow I could change this*, I think, watching my morning reflection unfurl in the mirror. My dark hair flickers in and out of Asianness.

If I believe my boyfriend has always possessed the language of love, I suddenly understand that I have assumed some dreadful feminine responsibility for it. It was always there inside of me, I see now in the mirror, real and heavy as blood, just waiting to come out. To bud.

Joseph's last weekend in Seoul we spend at the emergency room where I am violently ill from splurging on a chicken wrap sandwich at a TGIF. I had chosen Seoul ostensibly because it is the capital and because it is impressive and because it has the best museums, though in reality I chose it because it will give us the most anonymity. On so many street corners here you can see them: foreigners on their way to work with briefcases and backpacks and cell phones; foreigners with Korean friends or students; foreigners with other foreigners on their way to lunch; foreigners just by themselves, traveling alone in this vast city.

I had no desire to eat at the TGIF, but I remembered from a previous visit how many Americans were at the bar or with Korean friends, laughing and drinking.

But about an hour after the chicken wrap, back at our *yogwan*, I went to the bathroom and didn't emerge for half an hour. Another hour passed while Joseph and I debated my symptoms, until I could barely move without vomiting. The middle-aged *yogwan* manager called an ambulance and sat with me, rubbing my back and pinching my palm like an acupuncturist to stop my stomach contractions. When the men helped me into the little white car she stood at the door waving anxiously. She likes us because I speak Korean, because Joseph, as she whispered to me in the hall, is so handsome.

But here at the hospital none of this seems to help. "I can't get the nurse to come over," Joseph mutters. His eyes are panicked and he shakes me a little on the cot they've positioned me on. "What do I say?"

I roll onto my side and glare at the receptionist's station. Three nurses stand before it, glued there with what looks like shock. None of them can speak English.

Nurse! I call out in Korean. *Look at this!* Then I vomit directly onto the floor.

Soon I am covered with nurses grimly trying to stuff a plastic bag around my face so that I can vomit into it. Instead they are suffocating me and so I claw at their shoulders while Joseph tries to pry one off me. When he succeeds, the nurses hustle away, looking angry as well as terrified. I can speak Korean, but I am also very messy.

Another hour passes. Joseph is afraid that I will faint and leave him here, stranded and without the language. He is afraid they will put something in me he can't identify or, worse, withhold something from me that I need. He stands by my bed, stroking my hair and handing me the plastic bag to vomit in, patiently walking me to the toilet for my diarrhea. A Buddhist nun lies silently across from me which, as I swim up and up out of my dehydrated haze, amazes me since I overheard the nurse say she accidentally ate glass.

"It must have been that white food," I burble, referring to the chicken on the pale tortilla. But Joseph mistakes me and grimaces. "It was probably the squid," he says darkly. I buckle with nausea again and aim for his shoes.

After a few minutes a nurse approaches and asks me questions in Korean. I tell her my name, occupation, insurance number, and list my symptoms. She glances at Joseph. *Imshin?* she asks. Pregnant. *Anyo.* No.

She has already determined we are not married; she glances at my hand, at Joseph's hand and then back at mine. *Imshin?* she hisses again.

Anyo!

She purses her lips. She walks back to the desk and watches us. I can imagine she might be touched or amazed by what she sees: this good man watching over the hideous, vomiting mass of his girlfriend hour after hour so she will not be alone. The nun has no companions to wait with her; not even the car accident lying on his blood-spattered bed and wailing like a siren has a visitor. We may be romantic or just comic. Regardless, we are her freaks for the evening and the nurses from the other wards occasionally come down to catch a peek of us whispering to each other in English.

At dawn I am rehydrated from the IV. The nurse hands me a bag of blue medications with complicated instructions on how and when to take them. Feeling skinned, I nod and wobble outside on the arm of Joseph, who looks relieved the night is over.

"Why do they keep staring at us?" he asks.

"Because we're so good-looking," I reply, picking at a crust of vomit on my shirt.

"It's like being famous," he says. "That's us: almost famous."

My every nerve feels stripped, like radio wire. To touch my

skin would be like rubbing the edges of razor blades against it. "I guess that's why some men never leave," I tell him.

"Or some women," he says, looking at me carefully. And now I understand that this is what his trip has been about: to see if I will come back to America for him. His eyes are kind and tired.

"Not them," I reply. "The women always leave."

Snap snap. We wheel around and see one of the nurses tucking away her camera. She looks guiltily at us for wanting to take this picture: the white couple at dawn, the man's arm clipped dutifully to his girlfriend's waist.

I'll bet in this photo you can see us in the sun's half-light, shy and unsmiling. We might look a little hunted, our eyes dark and hooded from lack of sleep. Or perhaps we just look pleased, relieved as we slip out into the morning.

There is a commonly used word in Korean to describe the ideal woman: *chamhada*—literally to "be nice and pretty, modest, good-tempered, tidy and calm." Some of my Korean coteachers have even translated it as "purity." It's a word my students first taught me as both an insult and a compliment. "She's very *chamhada*," one student said, pointing down the hallway at a girl walking meekly behind her friends. She made a face, disgusted by the word's connotations.

Young Korean women I know are both *chamhada* and not, compared with young American women. It is impossible for me to tell if this is why certain male friends of mine all but lick their lips in the proximity of Korean coeds or whether it is the simple fact that, yes, these women are beautiful.

It's the question my Chinese-American mother insists she never had to answer with my white father. She knew why he loved her from the start: her strong opinions, her energy and slender calves. But perhaps desire has its own language, a vocabulary that empowers certain perspectives. If romance and love in Korea are spoken about, even whimsically, in English, how can that not privilege the native speaker on foreign ground? How can that not force its listener—its subject, really—into feeling manipulated? And if even part of the language of beauty comes in advertisements and films from someplace else, like the transplanted limb from a flowering plant, how can that not help but put a certain strain on interracial desire? Joseph and I walk out into the crowd, and our whiteness is a screen on which my students may play out their fantasies of America and themselves in love. But now I realize that it is also a screen for us. We project outward through it, loving the audience in the dark theater that applauds for us, that makes us feel, if just for a moment, admirable.

Perhaps my students want Joseph to enumerate the ways in which he loves me so that they can put themselves vicariously in my place. I am young and female and half-Chinese, almost young enough and Asian enough to be like them. But now I think that they just wanted me to be happy, the way Joseph wants me to be happy. And, I realize, I am happy. Many of my fears about race and loving Joseph are irrelevant: they have not and will not come true. It is not because aspects of the fetishist-white-man / docile-Asian-woman stereotype do not exist in the world and do not deserve to be reviled; it is because these aspects do not exist for Joseph and me. I need to let myself see this. I need to separate us from what is turning into paranoia.

Joseph's last day in Korea we spend at the beautiful ancient palace in northern Seoul with its secret garden. The palace is walled in and contains several long, one-storied buildings arranged symmetrically across the grounds. The main hall is painted dark red, filled with gold Buddhas and scrolls that are difficult to make out in the dark. We squint on the steps of the hall in the sunlight, wander across an enormous dirt courtyard to take photographs. To the far west are servants' quarters: unpainted wood rooms with rice paper screens gracing each doorway.

The palace is a miracle of stubbornness. The flowering grounds and buildings have been burned to the ground not once but three times, twice by the Japanese. There is an air of triumph to the tour guide's narration of this fact. She looks proudly at the maze of red buildings with their darker red tile roofs that snake over the slight crest of hill. "Koreans revere what is Korean," she announces. "This building will always survive."

Joseph urges me to sip again from the flat ginger ale I carry, warning me against becoming further dehydrated. He has been solicitous all day, trying to order in cafés and restaurants, counting out his bills so painfully the owner of one place finally reached over and took the money from him, wordlessly handing him back change. Joseph also undertook the Herculean task of cleaning the bathroom. I stood in the shower, almost weeping with gratitude as water hit my skin. And now we sit beneath the trees the tour guide instructs are jujube, their palm-shaped leaves filtering the sunlight out in long fingers over our faces.

Tourists wander in couples through the wooded paths to find the blue pagoda, disappearing, reappearing, disappearing.

"You are very good to me," I tell Joseph and, for the first time, lean willingly against his shoulder. Outside this place is the long block of movie theaters, their pinups painted in garish colors as large as the face of a building. Green buses flash by filled with college students, masses of girls with dyed red hair, boys with their Brando slouches. Inside it is just us. He reaches over and kisses my forehead.

"I'm going to get another soda for you," he says. He walks past a group of Koreans snapping photos of themselves beside the square lily-covered pool. He turns and gives me a goofy little wave behind them, shading his eyes from the sun.

Seeing his back turned to me in the sunlight, I sit and feel myself cracking apart. Maybe, just a little, flowering.

Sharks

My mother and father are fighting, Christmas Eve. Actually, it's
my mother versus my father and me, each of us having made some
drastically wrong choices regarding Christmas. For example: my
father, obsessed with evolutionary psychology this year, forgets to
buy gifts until the last possible minute, asks my mom to help wrap
the most bulky of his sadly mischosen purchases. He excuses himself via a certain male gene that is evidently not designed to shop
or use tape dispensers. I, nine years old, spend the holidays upstairs
in bed, reading, forgetting to empty the overflowing dishwasher, to
vacuum. We should probably be more contrite but, frankly, we dis-
appoint like this every holiday season. I doze upstairs and listen to
my mother's Hoover whine above the gritting of her teeth.

Now we are at my father's mother's house: Grandma Ilene's.
Grandma Ilene comes from Norwegian stock and, like her parents
before her, spent years in Alaska commercial fishing. Her small,

mint-colored house is filled with ink drawings of Ketchikan as well as needlepoint renditions of famous paintings she stitches for a hobby: Renoir's country couple dancing, a medieval tapestry fragment of a virgin with her unicorn. My parents and I are sitting under the unicorn, pretending to be speaking to one another. In fact, my father and I are speaking; it's my mother who refuses to register our sound waves on her radar. But wineglasses are passed, shrimp in garlic and oil sauce is spooned out on crackers, and tall, broad-shouldered Uncle Johnny, my grandma Ilene's older brother whose pink nose droops farther and farther down his face each year, tells my favorite story.

There are sharks in the waters of Alaska, he begins, and it no longer matters how much lethal silence radiates from the couch and the needlepoint scenes above it to liquefy me. There are sharks in the waters of Alaska, blue-finned, their fleshy white mouths filled with spear points. They circle the fishing boats Johnny and my grandmother and my father worked on. They smell the blood of fish hauled up in their rope nets. They feed on the viscera fishermen scoop out from their chosen catch, then throw back into the ocean. The ship rocks and wheels under the fishermen's rubber boots, while waves of water—sometimes up to twenty-five feet— crash over the bow. Everyone is nauseous except the sharks, who feed and feed, churning the rarely still waters white with the speed of their tails.

This night it's calm. A fisherman plays the water with a hook, one with a strong curved blade that could (and did) slice a man's thumb off. The fisherman swirls the hook through the water now, stirring up sharks, shark stew. A small one scuds by too close to the boat and the fisherman hacks its head off. For fun. Nothing else to do. He calls to my uncle Johnny.

"There's a shark down there with his head that I cut off," he tells my uncle. He points to the white chin sinking into the now smoky water. Johnny watches the body sink beside it. Blue-white ringed with blood. Dark and darker. They wait and talk for a while, forget about it entirely, and that's when they see—

"The body!" I yell, unable to control myself any longer. He tells this story every year.

Yes, indeed. The body rises up, headless, Washington Irving's nightmare from the sea, circling and circling the boat the same way it did before it died. It skims the boat's white sides, bobs where its head got lost, sinks back into the black. Again. It rises again.

"How long?" I ask, but already I know the answer. Fifteen minutes at least. Sharks do not have sophisticated nerve endings. They cannot tell when they are wounded. Even dead, they travel the same path over and over, reproducing exactly their last patterns and behavior.

I look at my father, who is smiling benignly over his red wine. My mother grips a horrendous silver and blue package in her hand, smiling also, less benignly. I think about all those genes packed into our bodies, threads of human matter so tiny they can barely be seen in microscopes. I picture them netted tightly together in my shape, the way leaf veins hold the form of the leaf when the meat of it eventually desiccates, blows away. I want to travel down the length of the body's slender cables, through jungles of lymph and sparkling nerve endings, to navigate the waters of the lungs with sharklike intent. All those stories I could unravel, over and over. I will be an explorer! I bounce happily on the sofa.

My parents smile at me independently, do not include each other in this. Who cares. I tear into wrapped packages and listen to more stories of Alaska, a land so cold and wild, so unfathomable, few can travel there or penetrate its depths. Like the body, its waters are dark and filled with surprising bright bursts of organisms, silver-white, like sperm. It's here I plan to start, this story, my family, and its connections to the world. Then move outward, to history and meaning and place, all the human relationships I can think of. The weave of my mother into my father and me, the thumbprints of my father dusting over the images of us both.

Outside my grandmother's kitchen I spy on my parents as they stand beside the sink together, refilling their plates. They speak in low voices until my mother suddenly laughs, lunges over, viciously hugs my father's waist. They separate, seeing me in the doorway. They circle and circle.

St. Agatha

Agatha Kleeson enrolled in Domus Catholic Academy my sixth-grade year, arriving in thick blue kneesocks with white tennis shoes—fashion chaos according to the rich girls who snuck nylons into bookbags, or wore bobby socks with powder blue pom-poms stitched at the ankle. This was bad; even though we all wore uniforms, we knew the rules. I watched as she laid out her books on her desk, each one covered with a crisp paper grocery bag. She seemed oblivious to her own lack of beribboned hair clips and contact lenses: she had the same enormous pink-framed glasses I wore and I was definitely not popular. After some time of staring at her I thought she appeared more horse than human with her long, equine face and square front teeth. I noticed she had a little nub of pink, glistening skin attached between her gum and the inside of her lip. It flashed out when Agatha grinned nervously at our teacher. And Agatha was black. The first one in our class.

"Hey," I said in lunch line. She turned and blinked at me. Now I could see that it had gotten serious: she had on a Peter Pan shirt underneath her blue sweater, stiff and bubble-edged. "Your shirt's wrong," I told her.

She blinked again. "What's wrong with it?" she asked.

"You need an Izod, not a Peter Pan," I said. "No one wears Peter Pans."

"What's an Izod?" she asked. *Oh man*, I thought. But I saw a dribble of gold necklace behind her sweater just then and pointed. "That's OK," I said. She pulled the chain out of her collar to show me a gold fan. "My uncles gave it to me," Agatha said, turning the little fan. "You want it?"

I held out my hand. I took the necklace home and later showed it to my mother, who insisted I give it back.

"There's no such thing as a friendship gift," she said when I protested. "No one buys you."

"I have to give this back," I told Agatha the next day, sadly palming over into her hand the delicate fan, its puddle of chain. "My mother says you can't buy friendship with a necklace."

"You want something else?" Agatha replied.

She had a throaty, piercing laugh, I learned. It sounded manic, the warbling giggle of someone drunk or insane. In chapel I would sit beside her furiously whispering jokes, but she never laughed in the presence of nuns.

The nuns were a hangover from Domus's founding days. This is all I knew about them. I wasn't Catholic but Agatha was. I had been sent to Domus after my mother—a lapsed Baptist—found out that I'd be bused to the south part of Seattle, where the schools were bad. My father was an atheist but he went along with the plan mostly because he found it amusing. Every night when I came home he would ask what I'd learned in religion class. I had been going to Domus for six years now and, because I never went to church with my parents or to Sunday school, most of the references my teachers made were lost on me. I spent my time in religion trying to realign the names of the Holy Trinity and its accompanying prophets with stories I had learned in mythology. Was Mary Hera? Was Jesus Apollo? To my father, quietly, I would list off a few of the saints and something about a resurrection. This delighted him. "Wrong!" he would exclaim. "It's all wrong!" Then he would lecture me about a man named Mill who said something about its being foolish to worship gods who didn't share our morality. I nodded. I didn't know what the hell he was talking about.

Agatha was the first person to tell me that Communion was not a snack. Before her I had understood God to be like gravity or the more boring facts of history: likely, but dull. With Agatha I could see belief, a process of faith requiring passion. Certain things in life are always true, she told me. But what if you find out that they aren't? I asked. That wouldn't happen, she assured me. You believe in them because they are always right. In chapel, I watched as her fingers wound softly into the chain with the gold Chinese fan. Watching the reflection of gold flicker across her neck, up toward her face, I felt something almost like envy. In class I stared, fascinated, at the walnut skin fading into the pink of her palm.

Because of her strict sense of right and wrong, in the beginning there were things Agatha wouldn't do. Curse, for example, smoke marijuana like the rougher students, brag about what she could steal. In class she sat with her head bent over her desk, silently working out sums or essay questions. When she got tired of this she would sigh at me and push back the tortoiseshell headband into her black curls relaxed with mysterious potions into a state of near liquidity. She stood several inches taller than me, had good manners and perfectly rounded breasts.

"Your friend is very mature," my mother said when I brought Agatha home.

Clothing, however, was beyond her. Agatha did not seem to feel shame for the navy pullover that daily grew more nubby, threadbare from the wash whose strong detergent I could perpetually smell on her. She didn't seem to understand how people saw her, and she always behaved a hair too awkwardly according to the social rules at Domus. I complained that she gave things to people too easily: sandwiches and jewelry, friendship beads on safety pins. At one point at her house I picked up a book she liked but hadn't finished and she immediately offered it to me. "What are you *thinking?*" I scolded.

"I can't help it," she said. "My mom tells me I should be like this."

"Your mom's white," I told her, as if I'd suddenly remembered it.

"Yeah," she said. "I know."

I spent the night over at her house often enough to notice. Her mother was white and her sixteen-year-old sister, Tina, was white and her uncles whom she adored were white. They all had the same light brown hair and hazel eyes, the same trim figures. Agatha explained to me that this was because they were "biologically similar." They even smelled the same.

Agatha did not smell similar. It wasn't bad, but it wasn't recognizable. I'd catch sharp whiffs of her when we sat together or brushed our teeth in the same sink. Sleeping over at her house, I noticed that her hair oil gave her pillowcases a yellowish cast where her hair lay, and glazed the top of her forehead with a sheen like sweat. She smelled both musky and clean: a trace scent of soap lingering behind the dark perfume of her hair.

Agatha also spoke differently from the way I thought black

people spoke on television. Agatha's speech and family reminded me of the white families on TV and at Domus who all spoke a certain way, asserted themselves through an insistently correct grammar what it was to be a normal child. Even Agatha's adopted family seemed normal to me, having grown up with the idea that a parent of some other race was not unusual and, in fact, not biologically impossible. Hadn't my mother, with her straight black Chinese hair and olive skin, given birth to me? And here I was: light brown hair, light brown eyes, already as tall at age eleven as my mother at thirty-nine.

I assumed that Agatha's white mother had carried Agatha for nine months; the adoption was a ruse, a common lie in reverse she had invented to explain away the embarrassing habits of her mother. The fact that she never mentioned who she thought her real parents were, where they lived or what they looked like, confirmed this for me. *If she's weird, don't worry, I'm not*, I assumed Agatha meant whenever she spoke (rarely) about her adoption. Or maybe it was like the story of Christ and Mary and the virgin birth, something I still had barely got a handle on at school. I shrugged and went back to lecturing her on her choice of bookbag. Adoption was something I had fantasized about for my own mother most of my recent life.

But Agatha's mother, I thought, looked very much like Agatha. She was of medium height, slim, with dark boyishly cut hair, and glasses in almost the exact style as Agatha's. Everyone in glasses looked alike to me, members of some outcast tribe distinguished not by coloring or height but poor eyesight. It made Agatha her real daughter, I thought, as real as her "biologically similar" child Tina, who did not have glasses and was very beautiful. Upon my arrival at Agatha's house, Tina would trot downstairs in navy leg warmers and tight jeans, brushing out her long hair. "Hi!" she'd chirp. She beamed at Agatha, Agatha beamed back. After spending a lot of time at other people's houses, it seemed odd to see family members so happy with one another.

At Agatha's, we wandered through the scorched grasses of neighbor's yards, past junked or half-built cars, peeling shotgun houses, boys or old women at their porches and open windows.

"You be careful here," my mother warned each time before dropping me off. "You listen to Agatha's mother and don't go where she says you can't."

"Of course," I replied. But when my mother pulled out of the driveway, quickly locking the passenger door, I went everywhere. And everywhere I noticed certain strange, sidelong looks that followed Agatha; hard, onyx stares when Agatha's mother called us home. *Something must be wrong,* I thought to myself. I just couldn't see what it was.

It was the year our science teacher locked our whole grade in the lab at school to watch *The Silent Scream* and classmates started "going together": a term blissfully ambiguous in its meaning as to the exact relationship between boys and girls. Todd, a blond boy who spattered saliva when he talked, had liked me for years. Now he wanted to go with Agatha.

"He can't!" I complained in the bathroom to Kirsten. "Why?" she asked. I thought for a moment. I had just watched *Live and Let Die* on television and seen Roger Moore burst from the Jamaican jungle hand in hand with a tall, dark-skinned black woman. After killing the hit men, he had tumbled the woman into the tall grass by a river, purring into her ear like a jungle cat. I remember the shock, the almost visceral horror I felt seeing his mouth cover hers, his white hand sliding over her dark, uncovered hip.

My father had sat on the couch next to me, chewing contentedly on a sandwich. "Is that *right?*" I wanted to ask but stopped. At that moment I suddenly knew what I wanted to know was unaskable. It was shameful both to fear and, somehow, not to; my first private emotion. Agatha had seen my parents together. She had often said that she thought I was lucky, though I wasn't sure what she meant by this. Was it because my parents, of two different races, were married and happy together, like Agatha and her mother seemed happy together? Why would it disgust me more to see a white man kiss a black woman than to see my white father kiss my Chinese mother? "How could he?" I wanted to ask my father, my stomach icy with nausea. Even when Roger Moore ended up with the white heroine, I couldn't erase that feeling of having been disillusioned, a little afraid.

At school I watched Agatha laugh as Todd chased her on the playground, his almost-white hair flashing. I stood next to her in the bathroom while she applied colorless gloss to her lips, then borrowed her tube and mimicked her. Her body was straight yet womanish, her breasts larger and leg skin—unlike mine—smooth and unscathed.

"Why?" Kirsten repeated impatiently, and when I didn't answer she assumed it was because I liked Todd myself. Agatha and Todd started going together that year, and part of the next, and they most likely would have remained sweethearts for years if what happened hadn't. He loved her. Years later, when we were in college, he called me up to find out where she'd disappeared to.

"I have no idea," I said.

"I sometimes dream she's coming back," he told me. "You know, she was my first real girlfriend."

I didn't say anything. I couldn't tell him I also dreamed she was coming back into my life and that I'd wake up each time nervous and afraid.

"I'm sure she's long gone," I told him instead. I didn't clarify this. He knew I meant "Good riddance."

On certain Saturdays that year, my mother dragged me with her to relatives' or friends' birthday parties, wearing me out with her insistence that I accompany her and a gift to each foreign living room. We'd show up on strangers' porches, my mother smiling in her best dress with a well-wrapped package in hand, me in tow, sulking behind.

"Cindy!" the Chinese women at the party would exclaim at the sight of my mother. Then I would be let loose to join the children down the hall, in the basement, by the pool. This Saturday we went to my distant cousin Peter's house. He was my age exactly and he frowned when his mother told him to introduce me.

"This is my cousin," muttered Peter glumly in the rec room. The Chinese children stared and snickered.

"She's white." A girl whose head barely reached my shoulder came and stared at me.

"That's not right. They don't look the same. They're obviously not related."

"My mother's related to Peter's mom," I said. "Auntie Jean is her cousin."

"Bullshit!" they chorused. Upstairs, my mother laughed with her friends and the sound traveled down to me as if I were standing at the bottom of an ocean.

Peter shrugged. "Don't ask me," he said.

"Is she adopted?"

"I don't know," Peter whined. "Just shut up about it."

The small girl who had been scrutinizing me came forward then and looked me square in the face.

"You want to play a game?" she asked.

"Sure," I replied nervously.

She cut her eyes to two boys sitting on the couch by the TV. "One of them wants to kiss you," she said. "Go outside and wait."

"Yuck," muttered one of the boys. He was wearing a plaid rugby shirt.

"Yuck," I repeated back. "I'll stay here."

The small girl sighed. "Just go outside," she wheedled. "Just for a minute."

I looked outside to see gray sky above an empty swimming pool. Small potted trees surrounded the deck. I made an unconvincing move toward the door and the girl followed me. "Go," she urged. I opened the door, knowing even as I did it I was making a mistake.

"Now!" the girl yelped. Someone pushed me and I stumbled out onto the pool deck. The glass doors clicked closed, locked by the boy in the rugby shirt. He grinned through the glass at me.

When I turned I watched another girl about my age wearing glasses and oversized blue overalls materialize behind the potted trees. She had lank hair and terrible acne. "Hi," she said miserably.

The rest of the party we walked around the outdoor pool and grounds together, commenting on how dumb it is to have an outdoor swimming pool in a city where it rains all the time. We tried to go back inside, but the glass doors remained locked.

When Peter opened them, it was to tell me my mother wanted me. He led me slowly upstairs, trying to seem as if there were another, more important reason for walking into the living room with me.

"Did you have a good time?" my mother asked. I leaned against her comfortable body. I nodded and thanked Aunt Jean.

"Your daughter's so tall!" one of the many birdlike women gushed from a couch, but something in her voice reminded me of the small girl downstairs. I avoided the woman's eyes as she showered me with compliments.

"So tall, so lovely she's going to be when she grows up! Don't you think, Jean?" But Jean just nodded in silence, walking my mother and me to the front door rapidly, as if she couldn't wait to see us go.

Paula, Monique and Gia had known one another from the same neighborhood, they said, their houses just a few blocks down from Agatha's. Like Agatha, the girls were black, but besides that they had nothing in common with her. When they arrived at Domus in the seventh grade, Paula and Gia soon became the darlings of Domus's white all-girl's basketball team with their similar lanky bodies, taller than all the other girls in our grade. Gia had thick, sooty lashes and a smooth round forehead made rounder by the fact she always wore her hair tightly pulled back. Paula in comparison was darker-complected, with a strange, slurred voice as if she had cut her tongue. Monique, however, was the most physically and personally impressive of the three. She wore her skirts short and never put on a sweater. Her white shirts always seemed to strain against her breasts. She was stocky and loud, her hair done in rows and rows of little braids that ended in blue and white beads that matched Domus's school uniform colors.

"What the *hell* are you looking at?" she asked me her first day in the hall.

By one-fifteen Monique had beaten Dave Weyman into a bloody smear on the playground; he had complained to the history teacher that she had taken his book. At the bus stop a block from school later, she pushed him down again, mounted his chest like a jockey and sat on him until he cried into the pavement. When she got up, Agatha and I watched Dave swipe at his red face with his sweater sleeve. Unfortunately, a secretary saw the incident and reported us. Because we were acting up, the science teacher told us the next day that we were all going to watch *The Silent Scream* again. In class Monique gave us a half-lidded sneer.

Before Monique, Paula and Gia arrived, all of us in Domus Academy knew the rules: no pitched battles, no hitting. If we had a problem, we bickered like middle-aged butlers at a tea party. Meanwhile, Monique called Paula and Gia her "niggers," Dave her "whipping boy" and "cracker." She pushed people in lines, tripped, slapped, punched like a boy. What scared us was the hitting. Unlike us, Monique wasn't afraid to fight. Meanwhile the Laurelhurst children spoke like television or radio announcers, their speech laced with tacit threats like doughnuts dusted with arsenic.

One day in music Monique walked up to the blackboard on which our homework was written and stood in front of it, blocking the assignment from view. The teacher had gone in search of the piano someone had again snuck into the boy's bathroom. It was hot outside and close to recess. The clock ticked as everyone waited patiently for Monique to finish copying, afraid to hurry her. Sun boiled through my plaid skirt, my oversize wool cardigan. Monique, indifferent, painfully scratched out the assignment from the blackboard, letter by letter. "Monique," I finally muttered. "Why don't you move, you big, fat cow."

Monique turned slowly. Behind me, I could hear Dave Weyman begin to sniffle.

"Who—said—that," Monique demanded. Her head revolved like a mall store video camera, capturing us all in her sights. "Who—said—that," she repeated. I could feel a teardrop of sweat leak down my collar.

"I did," Agatha said quietly when Monique's eyes settled on me. Monique stared at Agatha for a long time.

The bell rang and I shot out of my seat. Catching the sulfurous whiff of another fight, the rest of the class stampeded for safety like cattle in a thunderstorm. I couldn't stop trembling. But Agatha seemed calm even when Monique paced by us near the water fountain, giving us both the middle finger.

It was settled. I owed Agatha my life.

"Oreo," Monique said to Agatha the next day at lunch. She had been staring at her all morning, mouthing this word and others silently in class, rolling them around her tongue. She said it quietly now, as if testing a fragile toy. "Oreo. Running around like you wanna be white." She hissed, listening to Agatha give a book report in class. She couldn't stand Agatha's steady drone, her nubby sweater and uptight socks. She threatened to kill her after school.

I plotted hysterically in the washroom during break. How to get out of this? I panicked at the sink, hallucinating about Monique's powerful forearms, her legs as suddenly strong and thick as sides of beef. I thought about faking being sick. Agatha kept her fears to herself, however, and did not seek help. She reminded me about Dave Weyman.

"Nothing's going to happen," she assured me. "She can't hurt us. It's not right."

"That's stupid," I said, and rolled my eyes at her naiveté.

"You shouldn't let her talk to you like that," a sympathetic eighth-grader warned us in the hallway. "Just confront her, she's all talk." So Agatha and I strolled manfully into the cafeteria, deflating instantly like barometer balloons at the sight of Paula, Monique and Gia. I tugged Agatha back out into the hall. But Monique and her friends cornered us by the entrance and, coward that I was, I moved to the side for safety. When Monique began threatening Agatha, Agatha paused, tilted her head to the side. She seemed curious about what Monique said, turning and weighing each word for truth.

"You little nigger," Monique called her.

Our plan was simple. Agatha, to avoid Monique, Paula and Gia (who had, in our vocabulary over the course of the day, turned into MoniquePaulaandGia, an unholy trinity that always arrived accompanied by brimstone and fire) would walk half a mile away from school to another bus stop. Kirsten and I would follow for moral support, though we knew we couldn't save her. We were weak.

"Honky! Oreo!" the trio catcalled as Agatha, Kirsten and I trudged to our seats. Agatha sat silently, her hands folded on her lap as she stared out the window.

"Nigger!" Monique yelled. Agatha started thumbing through a notebook. Monique stalked down the swaying bus aisle, gripping every greasy pole between us. My hands had turned to sponges in my jacket pockets. I waited for the bus driver to say something, but he was miles away in his jouncing seat, daydreaming about a job that did not involve children.

Paula and Gia watched from the back scornfully as Monique edged closer and closer to us. It was the same expression they wore at the bus stop, at the school playground, in the half-empty hallway as Monique cursed, bumped Agatha out of the way with the weight of her enormous chest. Now Monique stood in front of us, her left hand gripping the last silver pole to steady herself as the bus lurched. "What the fuck is wrong with you, huh?" she said. "Didn't you hear me? Don't you answer me when I speak to you?" Her voice was so loud it did not seem to come from something as frail as vocal chords. "What the *fuck* is wrong with you?" Monique's braids rattled and snaked against one another. Agatha's gaze hardened.

"I seen you walking," Monique said. "At home. I seen your mother."

Agatha did not reply.

"I seen your sister, too. You don't got a father. You got a father?"

Kirsten and I practiced swallowing.

"Answer me, nigger. You got a father?"

Agatha shook her head. Her eyes looked swollen behind her glasses.

"No. I don't *think* so," Monique replied. "'Cause I *know* you. I *seen* you."

She kicked at Agatha's shin halfheartedly with her foot. Harder. That's when the bus driver finally woke up. "Hey!" he cried, as if surprised to find himself there. Monique's eyelids sank ominously as she walked back to her seat.

Every afternoon this happened. Some days Monique would be sick or we would get a ride home from school, or walk the several miles to the University District, and for one day or one hour Agatha would have a reprieve. It had gotten to the point where I couldn't even thank her for saving me; gratitude was too flimsy to a word. Agatha began wearing baggy clothes and sleeping in class. Finally summer came, releasing us from school. There were family vacations, picnics, sleepovers. Then Agatha disappeared. When she returned in the fall for eighth grade, age thirteen, her good humor seemed to have entirely dissolved. She moved listlessly and spoke as if drugged.

"My uncles are going to jail," she said when I asked what was wrong. "For antique fraud." I said nothing. I knew she adored her uncles. That night my mother called me into the living room when the story of Agatha's uncles was broadcast on television, showing them being taken, handcuffed, into court.

"Two Bellevue men are being tried today for running an antique fraud business that dates back more than ten years," the newscaster began, but I tuned her out. I focused instead on the faces of Agatha's uncles. They were still together, I noticed. Still brown-haired, brown-eyed, but, and it must have been the television lights or their brief time in lockup, their faces looked much paler than I remembered them being. They looked, I thought, incredibly white.

"I'm pregnant," Agatha whispered. It was November of eighth grade. I hadn't been invited over to her house for a month.

I nearly tipped my desk over in my haste to lean toward her. "You're what?"

"Pregnant. I didn't want to tell you before."

I watched our English teacher hand out new books. As she called the name of a student, he or she would rise glumly, depressed by the idea of more reading.

"How?"

Agatha smiled.

"I'm dating Michael Jackson's cousin," she said. It was the year that *Thriller* became the top rock album.

"Since when?"

"This summer. His name is Michael, too. He goes to Ballard High," she replied. I stared. *She's supposed to be in love with Todd,* I thought.

Over the week the story grew. "We're eloping," she bragged. "We're getting married, but we have to wait until I can get away from my mother. She doesn't want us to marry, the bitch." I noticed, suddenly, that her necklace had disappeared. Now she wore earrings, multiple circles of silver and gold laddering up her ears.

The next weeks more of our friends knew. We agreed not to believe her, but also not to say that we didn't believe her.

"We love each other so much! He's a lot handsomer than Michael Jackson," Agatha gushed. "And he's rich. We're going to move to Los Angeles."

"Does he sing?" I asked.

"He's making a record."

Kirsten shot me an ironic look as I chewed my thumb.

"Well, what are you going to name the baby, then?"

"Michael." Agatha laughed. "Don't be stupid."

Six months later her stomach was flat as my notebook. But her curly hair was longer and she wore thin, flashy jackets in steel gray or shiny black that looked as if they were designed by Martians. She stopped asking Kirstin and me over to her house, replacing this with a series of ritual phone calls to her friends each night after dinner. Todd, Jessica, Kirsten. I was the one she called first.

"I had a miscarriage," she whispered to me one Thursday on the phone. "My mother made me abort the child with a hanger. She's a fucking bitch! I was bleeding everywhere last night. I had to go to the hospital."

I looked at the peeling wall in my mother's study. The paint looked sticky and melting, the stained glass shards in the window like brilliant insects trapped in glue. "Agatha," I whispered. "Shouldn't you tell someone?"

"She and Tina make me sick!" Then softly, almost moaning to herself, she added, "My mom says I'm going to a foster home."

"You don't believe anything she says, do you?" Kirsten asked when I called her.

I didn't, though I wanted to. But it was too sudden and dramatic to understand. I had to see the foster home as a lie, a conscious rejection of her family on Agatha's part. But Agatha had even begun speaking of her uncles in the past tense, as if they belonged to another era that no longer existed. "I'm beyond all that," she would confidently proclaim during phone calls and at school, and I pictured Agatha on a train platform somewhere in flat prairie land, large steel boxes filled with memories disappearing into the distance. It didn't seem possible to think that there was suddenly this new Agatha crackling to life in the midst of what she had faithfully portrayed as herself to us. Yet, there was that Agatha, now there was this one. And somehow I had to believe in both of them. It was exciting in its way. In my mind I could see it: the dead baby in a circle of blood, the mother screaming with the clothes hanger. Agatha, drained and weak, stoically observing.

After two months Agatha decided to bring us proof of her affair and invited a tall, bald black boy from Ballard High School to pick her up from school. I gathered with Kirsten and Todd to watch this boy, this man, so much older than we were, so much larger than any teenager I'd seen before, walk onto our playground. He stood silently as Agatha ran toward him with her bookbag flying; his bald head looked pointed, bullet-shaped. He glared as girls, thin and blond, rushed past, their hands fluttering as they stared. Agatha seemed pleased with his disdain. She let him take her arm as he led her away.

"That's Michael Jackson's cousin?" I heard Todd ask. Kirsten shrugged.

"He doesn't look like him at all," Todd said. "Is he related by blood or by marriage?"

Kirsten and I turned to stare at him as we walked, slowly, away.

By spring Agatha had been set free of Monique, Paula and Gia. Monique, too, had heard the stories of Michael Jackson's cousin.

Now there was, if not friendship between them, an uneasy acceptance. They sat close together at school assemblies, nodded with their chins at each other on the playground. Hello. To me, Agatha became stranger and stranger. One day, Agatha came to school with her arm bandaged loosely. "He sprained my arm," she explained behind the swings. "He got jealous." Out came a story about another boy: a look, a word or two exchanged. It was after school and she'd been waiting for him by his car.

She plucked at the beige bandage as if it were a guitar string. I expected her arm to fly out of it, strong and sound. I expected the bandage to unravel, winding violently away from her limb like the cartoon of the Egyptian mummy. She said she let him do it, that she could have fought him but felt guilty. "It just seemed easier to let him," she said. "He felt better after he apologized." I watched her during the day as she bore this arm before her, gingerly, silencing even Monique with the fact of her injury.

In the past year she'd had sex with Michael Jackson's cousin as well as Michael Jackson, been pregnant twice and suffered an abortion and a miscarriage. Now she'd been hurt by a man. I tried to imagine what it would be like to be attacked by a boyfriend, but all I could think about was the way she described having sex, which sounded both grim and too romantic. "He stuck it in me," she told me once. "And then I thought I was going to die." I tried to picture the bullet-headed boyfriend wrenching her arm over another boy and how that would feel, how the fact she had given an arm for him might feel generous or cathartic, but I couldn't. She talked about how much closer they were since the incident, but I watched her wince in real pain at a sudden jostling in the hallway. "Sorry," I muttered. "Is there anything I can do?"

I remember that Agatha stared at me calmly then, slicing her eyes over my face. It was as if it were the first time she had ever taken me in, but she was not smiling. Over the last year and a half she had abandoned one by one all the things that had defined her belief in the world; I knew I was just another one to go. Suddenly angry, I thought that she seemed to be as much of an atheist as my father, dismissing anything that didn't make but the starkest sense to her. She was black, her mother was white and had adopted her, she told me. How could they get along? When she told me this earlier, I had thought it made each of these worlds exotic and exclusive territories and I felt left out. I didn't fit, really, into the white world and I certainly didn't want her to put me there as a way of letting me go. She was my friend. I didn't want her to hate me because she felt she had to—though if she couldn't get along with her white mother, how could she possibly get along with me? But, deeper down, I had always known I was part of that question. We had never really been close, because regardless of my own feelings I was part of a white world and she wasn't. *I* was the one who had always seen her blackness as exotic, dangerously exclusive. I had never let her forget that.

Agatha, silent, continued to stare at me. In two months she would be ratted out by another student for telling lies about her abortion. She would go to her first foster home, where she would live for a short, painful time. Then she would return, but would run away twice more. Once she even hit her mother so hard across the mouth that she'd split her lip, deep enough to need stitches. From that point on, Agatha would go to a succession of foster homes that provided greater or lesser support and leave each one cursing the circumstances of her adoption. She would get pregnant for real, not once but three times. She'd call up at odd hours of the night, alternately conversing in a strangely doped-up voice or raging. She'd even call me during high school using such vicious, obscene language I couldn't breathe while listening. "You cunt," she would seethe. "You yellow bitch." In two years more she'd disappear entirely except for these phone calls that would come for me, unannounced and without purpose, like oracles from the dead. "Why don't you tell Agatha off?" Kirsten demanded once. It had been years since Agatha and I had seen each other; still, there was her voice threading through the complicated nets of wires and pulses. I would listen to this disembodied rage filter through chains of phone connections without hanging up or stopping her steady, drugged stream of invective. "I can't," I told Kirsten. "I don't think she's talking to me."

But in eighth grade all this was still waiting to happen. I imagine my face in her eyes then: round and slightly too fleshy under the glasses and pale, my hair pulled back into a sagging ponytail. Agatha looked at me carefully, her appraisal done. "No," she said ironically. "I don't really think there's anything that *you* can do."

A week later her arm looked healed. The boyfriend appeared once more after school. Agatha ignored me in classes. At the end of eighth grade I would never see her again. But a decade later I would find a letter from her that my mother had clipped and saved. It would come from a community college newsletter my parents had received in the mail as part of a fund-raising campaign:

Thank you to the kind donators of the_____scholarship at my local community college. Seven years ago I found myself alone with no sense of direction. I was 15 years old, I wasn't living at home, and I was pregnant.

I enrolled at the college after realizing I needed a well-paying job. Without the scholarship money I could never have gotten through the nursing program nor looked after my kids properly. Few people these days seem to care or know how the general student struggles to make a successful future for himself. In my case, I had to think not only of my future, but my children's futures. We have all been blessed by the foundation's kindness. Now I can look forward to graduating in the spring.

Sincerely,

Agatha Williamson

The last name was different, but her photo was undeniable. Her hair was much longer now, I noticed, done in ropes and curlicues of tight braids. Her face and neck had thickened, making her look like a middle-aged woman. She barely smiled, though she looked content. But it was the glasses that caught me. Translucent and square-framed with the funny, dipping Z shape of the ear pieces. She still owned the same glasses denoting membership in our shared tribe, our nearsighted universe. Our childhood.

When I think about Agatha, I think about her generosity, how she protected me from Monique to her own psychological detriment, and I feel ashamed because I did nothing for her that was equally selfless. I have no idea whether Monique would have ignored Agatha those years if she hadn't spoken up for me. I have no idea if, left alone, Agatha would not one day have been forced into inventing a persona for herself that was half self-protective, half self-destructive. I am sure one day she would have had to come to terms with what it meant to be black in a white family and in a largely unsupportive white community. Whether it would have had the same effects on her life, I do not know. I do know that, when I would walk with Agatha around her block, she'd glance with guarded fascination at all the black families surrounding us. For all the hard looks that met us in our playing, equally hard looks were given back by Agatha, who may have known from the outset just what last happiness was missing from her life.

Perhaps Agatha's anger stemmed from feeling betrayed. What she trusted as true—mother, uncles, God, friends—turned out to be insubstantial as protection for her. What she believed was right and good did not stay that way for her, as it often does not stay that way for any of us, and maybe that was too painful in the end. For a while I thought that Agatha was unfairly denied familiarity in both senses: actual family and companions who resembled her. Who berated her in her neighborhood and at the bus stop? Who stood next to her, listening to Monique's berating? And who believed Agatha must behave according to certain rules regarding sexuality, love, desire? Perhaps Agatha's hatred for me grew from the fact that she knew I had boxes she as a black woman must fit into, while I disappeared into a white world without any apparent discord with my Chinese mother. After a while, her generosity itself seemed like a racist demand on my part, as if I had expected her to sacrifice things for me because she was black. Then I wondered whether her anger wasn't also because, defending me from Monique, she'd endured something I never could. Agatha, like Monique and Paula and Gia, lived in a world I simply could not comprehend.

When I think of Agatha, I imagine some quasi-spiritual guide—a childhood psychopomp—trapped in a world that smelled, like any playground, of wood chips and cold cement. Or perhaps something hotter: springtime in her neighborhood, where we wandered among the auto shops and the gardens scented with car grease and exhaust. We could hear the televisions behind the screen doors. We could watch the few teenagers catch and receive the same dilapidated football. Five blocks away was the beginning stretch of Pill Hill and the hospitals, and so there were sirens, too, the intermittent wails of someone else's disaster.

In one memory I have, Agatha stands in my foyer as my mother and father walk out of the kitchen to greet us. She fingers the skirt of her blue uniform as they introduce themselves and she shakes hands with them, formally. She smiles her gummy smile and they are charmed. We spend the night in my living room and she cannot help but turn to the photo of my parents and me together on their anniversary. "Weird dress," she says, pointing to me and my elated father and my mother smiling in her gold *cheongsam* that looks silver in the photo's black and white. But her voice catches and, for a moment, it sounds not so much like ridicule, but envy.

I do not remember what happens to the black woman in *Live and Let Die*. Around New Year's every year the same channel shows all the Bond movies in twenty-four-hour succession; I tried to catch it this year but, as I do every year, missed it. I can only recall that one scene now: the black woman under the white man by the river, the foliage half blocking their kiss. Anything else is speculation on my part. I assume she was killed in the movie—so many Bond women are—probably right after the love scene. I don't imagine her speaking.

How would she have sounded? I wonder. But when I try to picture it, Monique's own voice and form swim up before me, blocking the woman's lithe and darker figure. The woman becomes threatening then, not placating but bullying Bond away from their killers into this shaded place and, when he tries to take her, she takes him first: pushing him down, sitting on his chest so that he can't speak and struggles to breathe instead, feeling all that force on top of him.

In school Agatha and I had knelt together in chapel so that she could explain the service. "That's the Eucharist," she would tell me, pointing out the flat white disks in their dish. "Mary's the one in blue." I smelled her hair, warmed myself by moving closer. To our far left was the man-sized statue of Jesus after the Crucifixion, with his gore-stained palms and side. Agatha explained the wounds were the saving marks. "Saints have them," she whispered, and dug her index finger deep into her palm once to show me where the stigmata would come. I watched the blood retreat then quickly flush back to the white dent her own nail had made, darkening it, and imagined how it would look against her rib cage. In the movie, wasn't that how the Bond girl had died? The bullet into the side, tearing the flesh first a shocked white then bright red, the blood loosened in a stream like Christmas ribbon? I imagine it now: our hero stumbling off her as he backs away. It's only by accident she has saved him, of course, but he's still grateful. Or perhaps she's not mortally wounded. Look, now she's getting up as if to ask for help. He ignores this. Everywhere around them is the smell of iron and hair oil. He must leave; he cannot survive. There isn't time to watch her anymore, and so when he runs back into the protection of the forest, the camera follows, leaving her there, dying by the river.

Three

HUNTERS

AND

GATHERERS

Hunters and Gatherers

I'm six or younger, in the basement with my father, who has a BB gun propped against his thigh. Now he's placed it on my mother's stained-glass cutting table, among the slivers of red and gold and creamy white, long strings of black piping that look like iron but bend in my hand like fresh licorice. The gun is dark brown and seems very long. It isn't cold at all, since it's plastic except for the little brown-bronze hammer on top that snaps like a mousetrap when I yank on it. It isn't loaded—that's what my father tells me. "The gun isn't loaded," he says, "unless you hear it rattle." Once or twice when he hasn't been home I've gone into his study and found the gun propped nozzle-up in a corner of the glass deck doors, behind the dusty yellow curtains. It feels warm to the touch from being all day in the sun. When I pick it up and tilt it, the gun rattles: a black vial full of pellets. It's like the plastic wand my mother bought me at a fair, full of sparkling hearts and half moons, pink beads, little bells, glitter that drifts and collects like silt in the translucent corners when I shake it. I've seen the BBs he's loaded the gun with, however, and know these pellets don't resemble glitter or candy in the least, not in color nor in smell or texture.

My father is probably taking a break from writing his Ph.D. dissertation. He's at home all the time now, taking care of me ostensibly, mostly just puttering around his study writing about constitutional law. Actually, he's not even writing yet; he's gathering information. This is what he tells me when I ask: I'm gathering information on what I will write tomorrow. Tomorrow there are no pages. This seems to annoy my mother, who comes home from work sighing when she finds all those books still stacked according to size on his desk, each one sheeted with a fresh piece of typing paper. My mother works as a teacher for gifted students in a public school on the other side of Lake Washington. She is their only Chinese teacher. She likes it, but one night I hear her tell my father that *this was exactly* what PoPo expected would happen if my mother married an intellectual, and I'm not sure what that "exactly" means. My father, home alone with me, handing me a BB gun? When I ask my father how they met, he says they were in the same English class in college; my mother threw something at him to get his attention, a sharp comment, a book, he can't remember. Whatever it was, my father says he's still trying to catch it.

My father is a staunch libertarian, tall, thin, with dark brown hair and a dark brown beard, the fur as prickly as a bear's. He is always polite to everyone, especially my mother's mother, Po Po, who is always polite back, a sign my mother says isn't too bad. Before I was born, only Gung Gung invited my father to my grandparents' house. After I was born, Po Po relented, dug into her savings and bought my parents a dishwasher. My mother says that if I had been a boy, it would have been a car.

I touch the gun gingerly and watch my father clean his glasses with a yellow piece of cloth usually stored in the clapboard desk my mother's father built for him, another gift for my conception. Whenever my father gets bored with writing, he does this: cleans his glasses, comes out and finds me, offers me food I've already eaten or asks me questions I can't answer. He watches me with his head tilted to the side, like he can't quite place me.

Now he takes the gun out of my reach and lays it out on the table, explaining all its parts carefully. I don't listen, being more interested in what's under the table (a rabbit cage, old toys, glass cutters) and terrified of the basement, which is filled with hand-sized spiders. My father is trying to entertain me, however. He's telling me something about his father, a vicious Norwegian, an ex–bar fighter who killed three Kodiak bears with a single-shot up in Alaska. He worked as a hunting guide, my father tells me, and he'd shot the bears to protect some dentists he'd been hired to take into the wilderness.

"The dentists had seen the bears heading toward the river," my father says. "But they only had these flimsy little rifles." He gestures toward the BB gun wilting among the glass shards. "They missed the trio completely. Being dentists," he said, "evidently they'd learned only to work small."

My father offers to shoot the gun for me. "Do you want to see?" he asks. I look up from the cracked cement floor where spiders are sure to be pouring out at any minute. I nod. I picture brown bears lined up in threes outside the basement doorway, arms outstretched and ready to be knocked back by a spray of black beads. A girl at school has a mother who hunts, and in her foyer are the stuffed remains of her best kills: a pheasant, a deer's head, a brown bear rearing on its hind legs, its pink mouth slavering plastic.

My father picks up the gun. I change my mind immediately, but it's too late. My father is out the door of the basement with the gun and I know something will die. I can't conceive of a bullet entering empty space. I can't differentiate between what will barely kill a pigeon and what will kill a Kodiak. I have a sudden picture of my father's father—a man I will never meet because he's already dead—shooting things down, and me and my father and my mother trailing after him, like desolate retrievers, picking up the corpses of animals I know only in cartoon form: lions, lynxes, a deer.

When my father comes back I am sobbing. He sets the BB gun back down on the table and watches me, his nose pink from the cold, his head tilted again. "What are you crying for?" he asks, bewildered. As always, I don't know how to answer this. I keep crying, hiccuping on my own tears. "I didn't hit anything," he says, like I've accused him. "There's nothing here to shoot," he adds, but it's a complaint, not an assurance. He sighs, picks up the gun and goes upstairs. I follow. The gun gets put back in a cloud of dust behind the curtains and my father gets put back behind the desk. There are pages and pages to be written, in longhand, whole theories woven from the thousand little reference cards filed neatly in their green box. I go into the dark living room by myself to eat spoonfuls of peanut butter and cry myself to sleep. If my father's plan was to scare me off the gun, it works. I never touch a gun until I'm almost thirty.

At twenty-eight, I have this terrible idea. I'm going to write an article about learning how to hunt, but first I need to research it. I need to learn how to hunt. It's a terrible idea precisely because I have never had any impulse to hide out in a tree or swampy brush all day, waiting for something living to arrive so I can kill it. I want to hunt the way I want to jump out of a plane—I want the experience to be over so I can talk about it. Finally a friend with a .270 Winchester and a Colt handgun takes me out to a firing range to relieve me of my curiosity. The rifle jumps back and kicks me in the face, the handgun feels heavy as a slab of marble and just as slippery to hold. I become so scared reloading the finger-length bullets of the .270 that I shake. I have to sit down not only when firing the rifle, but when touching it as well.

"Great!" my dad says when I call him. He's just retired from a business job that he hated, a job that never required a Ph.D. Now he reads and studies Greek all day. Now he wants to tell me about hunting as a child out in the wilds of Bothell, Washington, where cats ran free as water. As a boy he studied taxidermy through a correspondence course, spent his Saturdays taking apart his kill, then doggedly putting the remains back together.

I am more interested in his father, a man I never knew. "Oh," my father says. So he tells me how his father left his mother for months at a time, drank, lived on a boat or some field in the Alaskan wilderness. Alaska was a refuge for his side of the family, he tells me, who turned to fishing and hunting for survival, drank hard and avoided the grunt work of canneries. He doesn't mention the Chinese, who worked there alongside the Norwegians early in the century. Po Po and Gung Gung once slaved in these canneries when they first met. My mother told me that story: how after their twelve-hour days of work, Gung Gung had given Po Po tennis lessons, the handles of their rackets smelling like fish scales.

Do you think your father ever met mom's parents? I ask. Not possible. He wouldn't have given them the time of day. Did he teach you how to hunt? No, I think I learned that by myself. I spent only one summer of my life with him, commercial fishing when I was sixteen. Is it true about the Kodiak? Oh, yes. That was the kind of man my father was.

My friend in Georgia takes me out to the range by the airport, settles the rifle butt gently into the little hollow under my collarbone, near the swell of my right breast. I still shake when I press my finger to the trigger. The shot goes out, a little wildly, but I get better. Each time my aim gets closer to the mark. Last week I couldn't get off the blank expanse of the target paper, but now I am firmly nestled in the black rings orbiting the bull's eye. I keep my eyes open when I fire: a great help. I make a note of this to write down later—I want all the minutiae recorded, stored up for when I write my article. My sights get better and better.

When was the last time you saw him? I asked. My father paused on the phone. That one summer, I think. He died after another weeklong binge. He fell into Sitka Bay and drowned, all his money with him.

Now my friend chooses a last sheet—the body target—pins it up and reels it out. This target is a series of black body outlines, like a man radiating images of other men out of himself. Each one is numbered in white. I look through my sights and picture him: the man's face down in the water, his month's pay floating around him like a wet green halo. From far away I can barely see what I'm aiming at, the delicate numbers drowned in all that black, but then I squint and find my mark, to the right, below the shoulder and aim there. For the first time I hit it dead on. The faint whorl indicating the heart.

A Tempest

In China, I finally lose it at the one good hotel in one of the last tiny stops before the last tiny stop to Tibet. I am on vacation before flying back to America after a year in Korea. I have been saving up for this trip since I first arrived in Asia; I told myself that I wanted to be prepared. But it is soon obvious to me that I am not prepared, not in language, patience or my ability to deal with the heat. It is summer, and the temperature has hovered for the past month around the 98-degree mark. Finding air-conditioning has become my primary concern, thus I have come here, to this hotel, to wait in a cool marble lobby in a cool stone building as I cash a simple traveler's check.

The hotel itself is shabbily elegant and looks like it had previously served as a governmental building; the façade still bears that square, dull cement face familiar to industrial Chinese architecture across contemporary China. Only the interior, currently under construction, suggests any kind of the lavish extras associated with good Western hotels: a plush red carpet runs up the wide steps, the brass around the concierge desk looks freshly polished. There is even a set of English-style floral sofas and padded chairs lurking comfortably near the glass entranceway between the sets of scaffolding unfolded by the doors. The hotel lacks enough wealthy guests to keep the building full. Thus it is converting what might have been a servant's wing into a set of very clean, very spare dormitory rooms. For six dollars a night you can shower, sleep on fresh sheets and watch bad subtitled Chinese soap operas on a fuzzy TV screen.

Backpackers on their way to Tibet are forced to stay in this renovated wing due to conflicting transportation schedules. The hotel has a steady stream of these scruffy Westerners who clash with the elegant surroundings. They parade through the lobby at all hours, stain the English sofa, blacken the red carpet or, like me, scream mindlessly at the concierge.

"Just exchange the fucking check!" I am yelling. The concierge, a very trim Chinese woman with the sourest expression I've ever seen, narrows her eyes and ignores me. The guard watches us like he's going to have to restrain me soon; indeed, he might. I have already thrown myself half over the marble countertop in a lunge for her attention. We have been arguing for the past half hour over a small mistake I'd made while signing my second-to-last traveler's check. In the line for the date I had accidentally written the wrong day. Scratching it out before the concierge, I rewrote the right one, signed my initials and handed it over with my passport.

"No good," she said immediately, handing it back.

"What do you mean? The date doesn't matter," I said. "It's me, look." I pointed to the signatures on both my passport and the check. She glanced at them but shook her head. "No good," she told me again.

After a month in China I am down to seventy dollars in two traveler's checks and roughly ten dollars in singles and assorted change to last me another few days. Working the black market for train tickets has delayed my stay out west by half a week; it is, I tried to explain to her, now imperative that I exchange the cash in order to buy part of a last-minute plane ride back to Beijing to catch my nonrefundable discounted flight back to Seoul. I am already over seventy-two hours by train away from the east coast. To miss this flight would be to doom me to a week's stay or longer in this town, fighting with the black market operators to buy exorbitantly priced tickets.

"You saw me sign it here; you can take it," I urged her. Her face grew small and sour-looking. She began, I realized with some amusement, actually to pout.

"No," she said again petulantly. "You give me another check."

"But this one's fine!" I cried. "Let me talk to the manager."

The concierge spoke in irritated Mandarin to a uniformed woman beside her. "She's not here," she finally said. "You must wait."

"Listen," I said impatiently, watching a group of sweaty older Chinese swing angrily through the glass lobby doors, arguing with one another, "another bank won't cash this because I signed it here. You saw me sign, you must cash it!" It was the "must," I realized instantly, that was wrong. The concierge's lips tightened.

"Please wait for the manager," she said.

"No," I replied. "I can't wait. I only have this one check. This is all the money I have; please, please, please exchange it!" The concierge shook her head and walked off, ignoring me. I did not budge. I began speaking to the other woman in my strange hash of

Cantonese and Mandarin and Korean. She, too, walked off. And so this is my present situation: no one behind the counter will help me. No one will speak or listen to me. I am, I understand, being shunned. This is when I lose it.

"Just give me the fucking money!" I yell again. She begins walking farther away. "You can fucking well hear me!" I shout at her retreating back. The sweaty Chinese men who had been arguing among themselves very heatedly stop and start watching me. "Fine! All right! Here!" I snap, and plunk down my last traveler's check. "Watch!" I sign it, date it correctly, and hand it over.

"You lied," the concierge says, narrowing her eyes and hissing. "You *lied* about the check."

"And you lied about not being able to change it, bitch," I hiss back.

Her pout turns into a ferocious scowl. She begins counting out money swiftly, violently, muttering in Chinese.

To say later, while tucking my money away, that I am embarrassed by my language and behavior is an understatement. I am mortified. On the street, alone, I avoid the stares of strangers as they pour and swirl around me in traffic, at the marketplace, at the movie theater. It was not, I keep explaining to myself, really her fault. Everyone is being taken advantage of here. I remember in Beijing haggling for twenty minutes over the price of a bottle of frozen water from a vendor stationed by the Forbidden City. An older Chinese man carefully watched me wheedle the vendor down to the price I wanted. When I got it, he clapped and cheered for me, as delighted as if the victory had been his own.

And the situation was comic, yes, I can see that, as well as recognize how it might be understandable given my situation. The unbearable heat here has caused the skin of my arms and stomach to break out into a constellation of red welts. I am frustrated by going farther and farther into the interior of China alone with little promise of returning to Beijing cheaply or in time. My moods have fluctuated wildly, my anxiety deepening as the trains I take rattle past gorse-covered valleys and red river banks, and the Chinese I see look increasingly mixed, foreign to the American concept of Chinese.

But even taking these things into consideration, my rudeness distresses me to the extent that I hesitate excusing it or being amused by it. The fact that I had known something like this would happen to me here, had indeed believed I would eventually crack under the strain of being in China, disappoints me intensely. I had wanted to surprise myself; not to be the person that I suspect I am. Traveling, I understand I do strange things. This I can accept. But as things get really ugly and I become increasingly angry, I worry in airports and back alleys and on solo mountain hikes, I just don't know if I can control myself anymore.

Rage is common in China. Especially in gang or family fights, especially when it is the middle of summer in the crowded part of town, in the crowded region of one of the most crowded countries in the world. Almost upon my arrival I saw Chinese pushing and shoving each other in lines, screaming into each other's faces so that spittle drizzled across each other's lips, striking their victims with canes and hats and bottles of frozen water sold from carts on every city block. "It's the heat," I hear some tourists say, irritable themselves as they drip sweat into their plates of sour fried rice. "It's the population," whispers the Spanish woman to me over the café menu. Panicked by the chopsticks, she'd asked me how I had learned to use such instruments.

"The Chinese are savages," she tells me now, watching two

old men howling at each other in the street. "They lie about everything here," she hisses, trying not to be overheard. "Don't you think
they are all liars?"

"I don't know," I say coldly. "I don't think so." But though I
glare at her, part of me finds her disgust amusing, her language
of dislike for the Chinese almost Shakespearean in its invective.
"Those nasty small eyes," she shivers, and I understand, even feel,
the same cultural nausea here. What did I learn about China,
growing up in America? Confucius. Dr. Fu Manchu. The horny
fingernails of the scholars.

"The Chinese race," Emerson once wrote, "managed to preserve to a hair for three or four thousand years the ugliest features
in the world." Riding my rented bike through Beijing, I examine
the bodies of the women: how the skin looks sallow and soft, like a
yeasty dough sweating in China's harsh sunlight. Their slight, almost
muscleless figures make them appear boneless next to Westerners,
their shoulders a little too rounded, the fat on the backs of their
arms a little too loose.

And on the trains, the strangers pressing, pressing. Their darker
hair, their eyes, their damp and amphibious-feeling skins blend into
one solid uniform: the Chinese, who recognize me as their own.

"Isn't she Chinese?" a young girl asks her mother as they stare
at me.

"You look Chinese," the matronly waitress clucks in the
restaurant I am at with a Danish traveler. Overwhelmed by the
language and the strange food, he lets me do all the talking. Com-
paring my darker appearance with his blond and undiluted West-
ernness, the waitress speaks only to me.

And the language. It bubbles up out of me. Guttural or singing,
a swift collection of monosyllables I recognize as the roots of the
Korean I've been studying, this language comes to me faster and
more instinctively than I would have dreamed. But my rising and

falling is more Cantonese than Mandarin; I am speaking a terrible Chinese triggered in a brain part only now unearthed, taught or reconstructed by these faceless teachers. Like a resuscitated grudge, this language oozes and seethes from my throat with impoliteness and anger. No one can really understand me—I can barely understand myself—but somehow the Chinese pretend to believe what I am saying *is* Chinese. "Where are you from?" they ask, and a few even look surprised to hear it's America.

And I can be savage, too. I jostle, I push. The language surprises me with words to ward off and defend, words to accuse, even, and threaten. "You taught me language, and my profit on't / Is, I know how to curse," Caliban spat at Prospero. And so I do, and so I learn watching two Chinese Muslims at a Xian mosque charge toward each other, screaming and swinging wildly. Men pour around them until the courtyard is filled with loose white cotton smocks like a band of clustering doves. They rip the men from each other's embrace, sneaking away the old one's cane, settling the younger one's white tatted cap back on his head. "It's fine, it's fine," they say, trying to soothe them. But they can't. The sun beats down, dust smears into the creases around our eyes, the few trees and the beautiful ancient wood mosque carved all over with swirls of Arabic and Chinese seem obliterated by the iron scaffolding that jigsaws into the sky from next door: the modernization of China in boxy, Western façades.

"The Chinese are frustrated by China just as much as we are," an American student living in Beijing tells me over dinner. "Tourists get overcharged or lied to during their vacations, but the Chinese are being taken advantage of daily. They're angry. Sometimes this breaks out in violence."

"I'm studying in China for the semester," I overhear another woman a few seats down from us say to a young Israeli man. He has, I've heard rumored, just finished his term in the Army. His hair is shaved so close the blondish stubble resembles duck fuzz. His wild blue eyes look even wilder at this woman's admission. "*Why?*" he asks. "Why would you ever want to study *here?*"

"Why did you want to *come* here?" the woman snaps back.

The Israeli smirks a little and leans back, shrugging. "I needed to find some quiet for a while. I can see it was a mistake," he says, shaking his head. He snorts and repeats himself. "This whole place is a mistake."

When I decided to live in South Korea, I did so fully aware that I should've tried to live in mainland China. But what culture specific to me, I wondered, would I have gotten living in Beijing? My family, the Kan family, came from the small villages south of Canton. My grandmother, Po Po, herself was born in Ellensburg, Washington, but lived for ten years in Hong Kong with relatives after her father sent her and her mother away to protect them from the violence of the Seattle tongs: local Chinese labor unions that occasionally participated in brutal, internecine wars. Po Po later emigrated back to Seattle and bought passports and birth certificates for friends to come to the United States around the 1920s and '30s. It seems my Chinese family lived and traveled around China the way they lived and traveled around America: rootlessly, depending on the resources and loyalties of distant family connections. It helped them end up in places as diverse as New York, Chicago, fishing canneries in Alaska, Seattle beauty parlors, Mississippi. It would really be my grandfather, Gung Gung, whose family and language I would be in search of, but where, exactly, did his people originate? My uncle Karl went with Gung Gung to photograph his village almost two decades ago. As a child I wandered around the art gallery rooms, filled with the glossy, vivid pictures of what my mother claimed were our family's cultural life:

the woman with bound feet, the peasants with their mud-spattered clothes. "Is that Gung Gung's house?" I asked, wrinkling my nose. The photo I pointed to showed a woman in a bare hut. Light poured in across the picture by way of a rip in what looked to be thatch. The floor was bare and earthy. There was nothing in that house except an ancient woman sitting on a stool. "She's a hundred years old," my mother explained. *She looks it,* I thought.

"This isn't really his house," my mother told me. "Gung Gung was adopted by this woman as a baby because his real parents were starving. We don't know who our family really is."

So I decided to go to Korea. And yet I asked Po Po occasionally where Gung Gung's village could be found and, when questioned nervously by Korean friends whom I would be meeting in China, I told them I was staying with family. On one poorly drawn map of China I had tried to trace how I might find the town closest to the place Gung Gung was raised. I imagined him as an infant, wrapped in dirty clothes, handed squalling into the arms of a stranger for a handful of change.

But beneath, behind all this lust for family connection were real fears I had of going off the deep end in China—feeling disjointed, lost in a racial identity I was supposed to have and didn't, pressured perhaps to be more Chinese by friends familiar with my bloodline, what would a year in China trigger in me? What would it spew out or, worse, what would it bury more deeply? I had traveled enough before to see what happened when I felt overwhelmed. I watched myself become either suddenly obsessive or moody, subject to startlingly aggressive behaviors for no reason. Who *am* I? I wondered at these times. I was behaving like someone I didn't know, becoming more savage, I occasionally thought, by reacting instinctively to whatever pressures were inadvertently applied to my nationality, my person, my sex.

And yet, I realized, by not going to China I made myself indifferent to one of the most important things I had always believed and known about myself: I *am* half Chinese, and, through time and public scrutiny of my appearance, at heart I have come to believe I am and always was fully Chinese.

I have never told friends or family this because I know how ridiculous it sounds. My appearance can't justify it, my language and my values certainly don't. "You just feel more Chinese," friends would say, and they would be right. I know this; but I also know that if I am half white, that half I have been encouraged to perceive as lesser. Pictures and books from relatives, museum outings from school or with parents, revealed startlingly delicate women on startlingly delicate snuff bottles, graceful marble dragons wreathed in jade. I remember my mother's white silk tunic from China embroidered over with black and blue silk peonies. My Chinese blood has taken precedence in my private imaginings and reimaginings of myself for its inherent, if somewhat artificial or adopted, beauty. I am Chinese, and the importance of this grows the more I feel I am encouraged not to talk about it, not to think about it, not to invest it with any particular power or feeling.

"You should see your family in China," my Korean friends told me over the course of the year. I replied that I liked Asia as a whole—it didn't matter, really, in which country I lived. But the Koreans didn't like this. "You should see your family," they scolded. "Then you can appreciate how good it is to be Korean." I smiled at the joke but balked at the suggestion. I didn't want to look for the slim thread of my culture to validate my feelings about myself. I didn't want to know who I was, I thought and still think to myself seeing the leper on the Xian street corner, the legless man who'd cloaked his torso in black rubber, dragging himself down the street.

Stunted, violently deformed, his face sunbaked a bricky red, he crawled his way past me on the sidewalk, where I tried not to recoil. Because beside the silken emperor's gowns and the beautiful, crumbling Wall is this: the violence and the poverty of China. "[T]hese fellows you / Must know and own," Prospero said to Antonio, indicating his fools Trinculo and Stephano. "This thing of darkness," meaning Caliban, his dark and monstrous nature, "I acknowledge mine."

In one of the local antique streets of the town I come across a shop filled with carved ivory figurines and bits of fabulous hand-stitched silk, teapots chipped and broken, Mao's Little Red Books in various states of use. Worn and faded some of them, some of them looking completely new, the Little Red Books are stacked in piles along shelves or tossed carelessly into bins of objects the customer can rifle through, resurfacing in the wave of antique flotsam and jetsam with the determined buoyancy of cork. I had already bought one in Beijing. "*Shi*," the store owner says of the one I hold in my hand now. It is the Korean word for "poem," a word taken originally from Chinese. He goes on in Chinese to say they are Mao's poems, a sentence I miraculously understand through my study of Korean and repeat back to him in English, which he seems also miraculously to understand, and he nods at me as he hears it. This is the kind of odd, running dialogue I have with merchants and waitresses and strangers in China: they speak to me in Chinese as I translate simultaneously in English. Perhaps, because I am beginning to mimic their own rising and falling intonations, perhaps because the expression in my eyes is one of understanding and interest, they believe I get their meaning.

There is no reason that I should. The only times I heard Chinese as a child were at my grandparents' house each weekend, and then only in conversations between Gung Gung and Po Po, whose burbling snippets I can remember occasionally understanding and responding to in English. This experiment failed for the simple reason that, because they had both worked to erase the language from my mother's vocabulary, I never got enough practice in Chinese to learn.

Indeed, the only Chinese I grew up learning from them seemed frightening, private, angry. My grandparents spoke it to each other in front of the family whenever they argued or scolded; whenever other, older Chinese friends would drop by. It was in front of their own children or grandchildren they would remain subdued, handing us dishes of food politely in English, murmuring commands for us to follow. But in Chinese, emotions flowered more quickly and more vehemently. I remember seeing Po Po berate her husband from the kitchen in rapid Chinese, Gung Gung assenting from the living room in his low, almost moaning Cantonese while he sulked in his chair.

My own mother's rudimentary Chinese seemed to come in and out of fuzzy focus, sliding in her mind like a tuning dial on a radio. I remember once sitting at my grandparents' house with my mother, Po Po and a much older Chinese matron. Po Po's guest could speak no English and so my mother astonished me by translating her every word, effortlessly it seemed, as the woman addressed herself alternately to me and to my mother. As a child I could not believe my mother was understanding this. I could not believe she knew this secret, aggressive language only her parents spoke and, when our guest left and my mother and I remained quietly on the couch, I was oddly afraid of her.

Unlike Po Po, however, my mother would rarely express her anger in Chinese. Although she scolded me in Chinese in front of her own mother, calling me *kai nooey* (bad girl) at her parents' house, she would yell at me only in English at home. My mother's temper is legendary; as a child I gave her the nickname "Old Yeller" after watching the Disney movie. It seemed appropriate to her sudden rages, though I did not entirely understand how it might also apply to her race. At home during summer vacations from teaching, my mother would storm occasionally through rooms and parking lots, furious at something I said or did, vital information I didn't understand. One such night I was on the phone with a friend; it was dark outside and my father sat eating the remains of our dinner.

Suddenly our front door slammed open, nearly shattering its windows as my mother began shrieking. "Who," she screamed, "didn't leave the porch lights on!" She threw her bag down and kept yelling, higher and louder, repeating the phrase insistently. "Who didn't leave the porch lights on! Who didn't turn them on!"

I cowered behind the kitchen counter as my father calmed her. The lightbulb, he explained patiently, had simply burned out.

But usually when my mother became upset she would stop speaking entirely. Giving me the silent treatment as punishment proved effective; it dehumanized me, I felt, in the most fundamental way. I could speak and it was as if I babbled. I could placate, cry, wheedle, but all in words she refused to understand. Her silences occasionally stretched on for days according to the severity of the offense; to speak to us during these times, she herself was reduced to grunts; abrupt, almost animal forms of communication. "Mom," I would beg as a child, "just talk to me." But she wouldn't, she couldn't, I overheard her tell my father once, and later I learned not to ask.

My mother's silences—long, shunning silences—dominated me in a way physical punishment never could have. They brutalized, I felt, our relationship to each other. And yet I was temperamental, too. In fits of anger I broke vacuum cleaners and toaster ovens, threw dolls or dishes, got into random fights at school. "Temper, temper," the elderly woman down the block used to scold me as I played too roughly in her garden. But now when I'm angry, I find it impossible to confront the person verbally. I shrink from the person's company, avoid looking at his face. At times like these I know my language can only, will only, shut down.

Growing up, I knew I had a temper; it was partly inherited from my mother, I believed, who herself complained about Po Po who, when my mother was a girl, also used to fly into rages. From this I learned to identify my own worst behaviors as like my mother's and my mother's mother's; perhaps, because I eventually learned to see and recognize these women as Chinese, my understanding of my behavior and even my behavior itself became colored as well.

And yet their anger is deeply understandable to me. Po Po and my mother were full-time workers at the same time they raised their families; my mother had even begun her Ph.D. work in education when I was a girl, considerably amplifying her workload. If my mother's anger seemed random it was because the source was not always easily or individually identifiable; my father and I had over the course of time become mere drops of water in a sea of frustration that caused her to lash out at those close to her, her anger rising to fury in pitch and tone as nothing became easier. And if the vehemence of my mother's anger surprised me, it was because its nature was exactly and unnaturally opposite to the gentleness and tenderness—the poetry—that accompanied her. "You're my favorite child," my mother teasingly cooed at me, her only child, as she stroked my hair. On the street, walking with me, she winds her arm around my waist, places a hand gently on my back as she stands behind me in lines or at shop counters. My favorite picture of us together is a snapshot of us before a restaurant in Hong Kong. In it we stand side by side, our arms wrapped around each other where we can reach: mine around her shoulder, hers gently hugging my waist.

At times like these I understand how anger is a visitation, a strange bird come momentarily to roost. The real woman my mother is would live her whole life like this: smiling at me over the table, letting the dimmed restaurant lights spark jade gleams in her black eyes.

Growing up, I try to keep my temper under control; I try to be nice in any circumstance. But the natives are restless under my skin. The natives in me are wild. Once in Korea, I slapped one of my students. Yes, the school allows corporal punishment, even occasionally encourages it, but still I was shocked to see my hand raise swiftly toward the girl's unsuspecting face, to feel my fingers sharply bat her nose. Tears welled in her eyes. What had she done? Not spoken when I commanded? I walked around school feeling as if something had come loose inside me. I responded inappropriately to questions all week, laughed inordinately loud or was rudely silent, and once found myself yelling at a stranger offering me food. He had wanted, I realized too late, to be friendly.

I watch China slide by as I travel farther and farther west, abandoning the cities for the muddy fields, the odd cliffs with dwellings that look hacked out by hands or shards of crockery. I see cavernous entrances yawning from hillsides, scattered trash, families bathing by the river. Or neater rows of mud packed into labyrinthine walls to separate houses from houses. As the bus or train whisks by, I imagine I can even see the fingerprints packed into the muddy surfaces, row upon row, like the marks of large teeth.

There are cliffs, there is the Yangtze, brown and clotted in its filthiest cataracts. But the landscape is beautiful, as exotic and vast as I'd imagined it could be, and I am proud of it.

"The Chinese will take over the world," my mother jokingly claimed to me when I was a girl. But at school, and occasionally at family gatherings, I heard different stories: the Cultural Revolution, the tong wars that hurried the death of my great-grandfather, the great-uncle who made potions out of jujube leaves and swindled family members, the binding of women's feet till the toes rotted and dropped off. China was Communist, I learned at school, a fact that had unclear and frightening connotations for me. Weren't Communists liars, murderers of their own people? If China was attractive it was so only because it was exotic and dangerous, because it was not and never really would be me. I was a polite, good-natured, American child.

After a while, when my mother and family talked about the Chinese, I noticed that they spoke in two tenses: the distant past and the looming future. My mother liked hearkening back to a glorious Chinese history in which gunpowder, the stirrup, ice cream were all perpetually being invented. Hers was the China of Ming vases and Q'in dynasties, and when she published her coloring book for children, *Jing Ho Hauk Ho*, all the projects were for traditional Chinese games: dragon boats and silk ribbon batons and lion dances. Similarly, the future of my mother's China seemed wondrous, pristine and untouchable. There was nothing of the Cultural Revolution's violence, Communism's irrationality or Tiananmen's fascism. Po Po herself refused to go back to visit China, being singularly uninterested in travel, she said, or the progress of our family's homeland. Even Po Po's sister Opal, more adventurous by nature, shunned modern China for what she called its cultural backwardness.

My own experience of China's "backwardness" I had seen in

my neighborhood. A Cantonese family moved down the block when I was ten, and no one in our nearly all-white neighborhood knew what to do with them. The family could barely speak English and left strange, foul-smelling pots of unknown edibles brewing on their back porch. I had heard other children tell the family's oldest girl to "go back home on the boat"—something I knew I could never say myself—though I, too, was surprised by the fact she and her parents smelled differently, spoke rudely and too loud, spat on the street and dressed in brightly patterned clothes that never matched. My mother explained to me that they were probably from the country, certainly not from Beijing or Shanghai. Physically they looked like they came from southern peasant stock, like our family did, she told me, with their short bodies, round faces and slightly greasy skins. Like us, they lacked the high cheekbones and willowy figures of the elegant Mandarins from the North. My mother's tolerant yet slightly condescending tone as she said this suggested that this family didn't, couldn't, know any better. But weren't we, being also Cantonese, the same as them? From this I learned that there were parts of China that were barbaric and embarrassing and had nothing to do with the glorious past or future shimmering in my mother's imagination. Indeed, if any part of China was to be dismissed, it was the part of us that resembled our Cantonese neighbors: China's present. It was the worst example of what China could be to us, both politically and culturally. After a time, it even seemed to me that contemporary China was the worst *personal* representation of us as a family, and I generally avoided speaking about my biracialness. If, in grade school and high school, I was forced to discuss it, I very clearly told friends that Po Po and my mother had grown up in the United States. I never told anyone that they were Cantonese. I wanted to distance my family from the immigrants in my neighborhood and from what people saw on the news. As far as I was concerned, my Chi-

nese family was bred directly in the beds of ancient Mandarin offi-
cials, deposited here by liberal American, supernatural powers. It
made my family—and by association me—part of an adopted
mythology to be celebrated, revered, hopefully forgotten.

Obviously, traveling in China, I am conflicted as to what I feel
for the Chinese. Are they, despite my mother's joking claims to
racial superiority, the savages I once believed them—and me—to
have been? At times they are the example of what I love most
about my family, its strange exoticism and history. In a deserted
café I stop, exhausted from the heat, and drink a sweet pale juice
from a fruit whose name I cannot identify. I think of a college production of The Tempest I once saw, in which a black woman played
Caliban—not an unusual casting choice, since it is difficult not
to read The Tempest in light of later British imperialism—as a way
of critiquing our historical notion of savagery. But what struck
me was the woman's continuous crouching shuffle throughout
the play. While the white actors around her stood and walked normally, she had to scuttle on all fours, her head never extending
beyond the mid-thigh point on Prospero. She growled her singing,
poetic lines, often muddying the meaning because she spoke so
closely into her chest. How degrading! I thought, watching her.
Her being on all fours seemed to contradict what the director
wanted to tell us: that Caliban was unfairly subjugated by Prospero, that Caliban was his human equal. Instead the woman's
crouch told me that the native is the animal, no matter how justi-
fied her anger, how cultivated her speech.

And in the end, when everyone is reunited and goes home
happy, Caliban disappears rather than exits. She ends the play—
her play—in silence, dehumanized by the indifference of the
other characters to her plight. No one speaks to her after Prospero
passes judgment. She is beyond attention or language—the language she herself worked so hard to master. If in my mind's eye of

China I see myself or my family in the play at all, it is at this moment: stuck in a place that has confounded what we perceive to be ourselves, cheated out of a claim to cultural ownership, shunned. Caliban is savage because she is seen as savage and, in the end, it is almost impossible for her not to believe she is by nature that way, too.

I wonder what the black actress thought as she played her role. Did she, after weeks of rehearsal, come to hate her white costars? Did she come to hate herself, forced to crouch that way night after night? Did she see the play as a vindication of her race, her culture's history in America? Or did she suddenly start to obsess over her personal flaws, her little temper tantrums, her "not niceness" outside of the play? I see my mother's irascibility in me as much as I see her mouth in my lips' shape, her epicanthic fold in my eyelid, and believe that to change myself must be a physical as well as a spiritual act. "You are your father's daughter," my mother tells me. I praise silently the straight Nordic nose, the lines of my cheekbones—like good scaffolding—struggling under the weight of all that flesh. I tell my mother, "Yes, you're right, I am my father's daughter," but what I really mean is "Please, just make me less Chinese."

When I arrived in China the first thing I did besides find my hostel was spread out the guidebook's map and plan my itinerary. I circled the city names I wanted to visit, writing out what little information I could find regarding fare prices and train times onto a notebook sheet: Xian, Shanghai, Lan Zhou and the Tibetan outback, Tianjin, the far western Uighur Region. Then I looked farther along the southern part of the map, the crotch of Canton where Po Po told me Gung Gung had been raised: the family's wellspring of Chinese culture that could just as easily dry up as gush forth. I wandered along the streets of Tianjin, looking at the storefronts and cafés left strangely empty in the hottest part of the day. I had in my pocket a copy of Mao's Little Red Book, which I planned to give to my parents as a souvenir. For a moment, however, I wondered whether it was a good idea. My mother cannot read Chinese. The only person left in our family who can, since Gung Gung's death, is Po Po, and even she speaks and reads the language with less frequency, living now with one of her American sons who can not understand her, visited by family that has no real connection with the China of her husband.

After Gung Gung's death from cancer in 1985, I noticed he was rarely mentioned by my family. Po Po never discussed him unless asked; my mother made almost no reference to him. Nor did I. And it is now in China when I try to call to mind what Gung Gung had been like as a man—the handsome husband who drove a taxi for years and ran not one but two laundromats to care for his children—that he really disappears, falls silent. I can see the dark wings of his hair greased back, the high cheekbones of his face, but his *voice*—what he ever said directly to any of us—recedes like the hills of Lan Zhou from the window of a train.

My uncle David, my father's brother, once told me he had been impressed by Gung Gung's native intelligence, his self-taught facility with paintbrush and carpenter's tools, though saddened by the fact that all his life Gung Gung, like the parents of the Cantonese family in my neighborhood, could never express himself in English. Though he lived for fifty years in America, my grandfather never learned to speak English properly. I can imagine what my uncle David, a college professor, must have thought about this. My uncle David lives in Europe and directs operas; for him, Gung Gung's lack of fluency might have been, if certainly not a sign of backwardness, at least a tragic example of his perpetual displacement.

What surprised me when I learned this fact was that I had never noticed Gung Gung speaking brokenly before. I was slightly resentful that anyone should suggest he did. To me he had been as fluent as my father or mother, and so when my uncle David identified his speech as clumsy and his grammar barbaric I was as shocked as if someone had told me my father had really been speaking French to me all my life. I am shocked, realizing that for most of our family history Gung Gung had *actually* been silent; today, perhaps because I am aware of this, I cannot remember one speech he ever made to me, though we spent hours together at a time, though I remember the endless stream of toys and stamps and Chinese candies he presented me with. I remember standing with him in his basement workshop watching him build the shelves that lined my mother's walls at home. This was, I realize now, his way of conversing. I am intrigued by the fact that he was adopted as a baby, too; a symbol of not only his own displaced state in America, but perhaps his family's in China. I see him as a stranger washed up on two different shores and am sympathetic as to how he must have been represented, how my mother and Po Po might have sometimes railed at him to speak up and take his place in this new society. Perhaps, thinking about his death, my mother and grandmother cannot help but feel a little resentful, too, at his years of silence that have, over the course of time, only deepened from the grave. For years his acknowledgment of us was our acceptance into his love and culture. Without it, we were shunned. "It was upsetting," my uncle told me once, "watching your grandfather try to express himself. It wore him down. He grew quieter and quieter in any conversation."

In Tianjin, I came across new businesses with horseshoes of wreaths at the doorway, lucky red banners the color of my Mao book draped across the storefronts. But something about the lack of activity in these stores, compared with all the flowers and beautiful signs, made the places seem more like Chinese funerals than celebrations. Walking past them, I remembered the day we buried Gung Gung, the several wreaths at his own grave site. I was fifteen years old. I remember that I stood numbly with Po Po and my mother, watching the pastor read in English and Chinese until his youngest son, my uncle Karl, broke down. That's when we allowed ourselves to cry, all three of us then wordlessly, as the tears streamed into our open mouths.

I pass through the hotel two more times this afternoon while arranging my flight, both times avoiding the looks of the concierge behind the counter. They are deadly looks, and she's serious about watching my every misstep down her clean lobby. Chastened, I drag my backpack like a dead body past her desk. Crumbs of red dirt flake from my boots onto the floor's sparkling parquet. At least the guards have stationed themselves in a different corner and the group of Chinese men has gone. Only the tourists are left in ragged clumps, their heads pushed conspiratorially together.

Two of the tourists have come from the outlying areas of Tibet. Like me, they have just bought a plane ticket for the same flight to Beijing, so we arrange a bus trip to the airport, haul our bags out to wait for the conductor. On our last-ditch flight we sit together, excited and gregarious as the plane lurches heavily into the sky. I watch as they unwrap their souvenirs from soft cloths and mulberry paper for me to see. A prayer wheel, a knife, a bit of Tibetan banner.

Below us, clouds have wreathed the distant hills a light green that turns silver, then blue, then silver again. Small towns dot the mountainsides, mixing man with nature in vast disproportion: the landscape appears ready to devour the buildings sprouting hardily, almost desperately, out of it. "What did you find?" I asked my mother after her first trip here, when I was in high school. "I found out that I'm American," she answered.

I had expected a far more quotidian and concrete answer from her, such as a favorite building, a good restaurant. I had never thought of my mother as someone suffering an identity crisis before; now I cannot stop thinking of all the various identities she, or her own mother, or any stranger, possesses. Is the more important self to each the independent personality, or the public one? Are my mother and my mother's mother, as I hope I am, contented now by nature with only the odd stabs of anger and regret? Before, I had seen the self as seamless, a monochromatic piece of personality and emotion. Now I understood there could be gradations, finely demarcated areas between want, belief and feeling. Perhaps the self visits between them, resting its full weight only momentarily in one area or the other, making you or the world believe this one side of you—this slice alone—is all you really are.

The girl beside me is Canadian and seems very anxious about the security of our plane. We had both read in our guidebooks that Chinese airplanes tend to be older, poorly built Russian models. It was not uncommon, the books warned, for flights to go down. Better to get insurance.

So when we hit turbulence, the girl looks desperately at me as if I could do something. To distract us both I begin a halfhearted conversation about her trips around China, about my trips around China, about my experiences in Korea. "I used to carry around a little notebook in which I wrote down every Korean word and phrase I heard," I tell her and she looks at me then, sharply, as if I've revealed something too personal.

It is with great relief that we unbuckle our seat belts as the plane touches down, pulls sluggishly into the gate. "Do you think you'll stay on in China?" the Canadian girl asks me, but I tell her, "No, I must catch my flight back home to America." In the day left here I plan to bicycle through Beijing again. I plan to make one more trip around the shady neighborhoods of the Forbidden City, to watch the city dim at nightfall and turn into that familiar blanket of lights and neon all large cities become. "Don't you want to stay?" she asks, but I shake my head as I work my backpack out from under the seat. I've only been in China for a month, though it feels as if I've been here my whole life. I do not have the patience to stay. I do not have the need or will to belong here anymore, I tell myself, and so I shake my head at her again when she repeats her question, shoulder my bag and go.

Bad Vacation with Tasaday Tribe, or How My Grandfather Acquired the Laundromat

This is the story my Chinese mother told her white mother-in-law, Ilene.

In January 1942, my Chinese grandparents live in Seattle near Jackson Street in a slightly ramshackle, shotgun house. Po Po works in a sewing factory while my grandfather, a thin man whose stomach and arms are stringy with muscle, goes out every evening in his taxi to collect fares. It is a tiring job that he hates. Gung Gung's spoken English is not good though his comprehension is perfect; what irritates him about the job is picking up strangers who hear only his slurred and broken expressions, condescend, undertip. Night after night is the same thing: drunken couples wrestling off jackets and shoes in the back seat, sailors who dash from the cab to avoid paying, rich whites staring at him icily or, worse, rich Chinese who proselytize like itinerant preachers. Work hard, they tell him. Harder! You can get a better job than this! Gung Gung scowls and hunches a little farther over the steering wheel.

At this point he and Po Po have three children and are well on their way to a fourth, though they don't know it yet. They are incredibly poor, and the only thing that makes this knowledge bearable, forgettable, is that everyone around them is, too. Then came the war, the order for the Japanese to leave for internment camps, and Gung Gung suddenly is presented with an extraordinary business opportunity.

A man named Yanagiwa or Yamamoto (it is unclear, my mother said, the name anonymous with syllables) who lives on the same block comes to visit Gung Gung late one night a few days before Y. must go by train to the camps. He doesn't want the government to repossess everything, his home, his laundromat. So he offers my grandfather his business on Twenty-third Street for a dollar. A dollar, with the promise that my grandfather will give the laundromat back to him upon his return. He can keep the profits; Y. will even train Gung Gung how to run the machines. It is an offer my grandfather thinks over briefly at most. Who is this man? Why should he trust him? Y. waits patiently on his clean doorstep. "OK," Gung Gung tells him.

Y. and Gung Gung are not close. They are not, according to my mother, friends. They had seen each other once or twice around the block and spoken, of course. Perhaps they had gambled and/or drunk together at the occasional club in Chinatown, though the possibility of Gung Gung's having gotten to invite Y. into the house was unlikely because of Po Po. There were stories about things Japanese soldiers did to the Chinese in cities they conquered, Po Po knew, and perhaps it was these rumors that kept her quietly (or not so quietly) hostile, sympathetic to the Chinese who, during the thirties, put up signs in their storefronts indicating their ethnicity so as not to be mistaken. So Y.'s decision to trust

Gung Gung with the safekeeping of his laundromat would largely have been based upon my grandfather's open-mindedness, the appearance of honesty radiating out of his small, bright eyes. Or perhaps it was nothing more than that my grandfather was home that evening, sick with a head cold, his taxi cooling under the few stars out that night. This fact, and the fact that Gung Gung gave back the laundromat twenty years later (flourishing, and with a second laundry near the Bon Marché in downtown Seattle created from its profits) for the same price he'd been offered it, is what makes the story one of my family's best anecdotes.

Unfortunately it is untrue. Nothing like this ever happened.

Today I am swimming in the blue, blue waters circling the Philippines, one pink human jot in the amniotic sac of the world. I rock under a sky the color of chicory, watch my fingers turn to shrimp in the brine. At least I would like them to. But first I must get out of this bomb shelter masquerading as a youth hostel in Manila with my two friends intact, if not tactfully. We argue. For instance: Trecia is upset with me because I cannot say her name right.

"Tree-see-ah," Trecia snaps. "Not 'Treesha.' Why is it white people can never say it? Koreans say it right, black people say it right. Why can't white people?"

Julie glances smugly at us when she hears this. She who is indisputably white has always said Trecia's name correctly.

Trecia is charming, flirtatious, loyal and, at age twenty-four, very specific about lip liner and the color of her nails, though this week you wouldn't know it. Her sense of humor got misplaced along with her eye shadow somewhere in Manila. Like Julie and me, Trecia is living for a year in Korea on a Fulbright. She is toast-colored, round-faced, half black and half Korean. In Asia, however, Trecia is more impressed with being Korean than black, and has developed very strict standards about what might qualify a person for this category. White Julie is the one who normally fails; I, being half-Chinese, fail only 50 percent of the time. Trecia remembers this suddenly, switches gears. And Julie! She doesn't like the food, is tight-fisted, can't seem to pick up any language . . . I smile. Julie owes me four dollars.

Such a paltry sum would easily be forgotten were Trecia to ignore it, but the fact Julie refuses to pay it enrages her, deeply offends her ordered sense of the moral universe. Such stinginess would be unheard of in an Asian! Meanwhile, I sneak to the bathroom (kicking the chicken I find there out of the way) to secretly devour our last mango. Discovered, my treachery becomes no racial trait but a defect of birth order. "Only children are selfish," Trecia proclaims when she catches me pulp-handed, trying to hide the bonelike pit behind my back. "What is *wrong* with you people?"

To cheer us up, Julie unpacks the guidebook again with its pictures of white sand beaches, catamarans trailing off into jewel-toned waters. "Look where we're going," she croons. No more smog, no more guidebook-approved hostels with chickens. We will float in salty waters that lick our kneecaps and elbows, that lap the edges of our rib cages like so many velvet tongues.

"When we get there," I say, "I'm going to find a farmer's market."

"So you can get our last mangoes?" Trecia asks.

Now it is Julie's turn to smile. She is tall and lanky from years of training as a dancer, with a mass of black curls that shrink into a single dank weed when wet. Her mother is Austrian, and Julie has inherited her mother's broad, muscular features: the cheekbones, the browbone. Trecia is suspicious of Julie, partly because of these looks. This came about from a teachers' training exercise in which Julie's "students" (us) were supposed to tease her about her appearance. When a group of Korean-Americans said she looked like

Julia Roberts because of her name and hair, Julie retorted that, well, all Asians looked alike to her, too. "This connection between me and Julia Roberts is racist," she explained to a suddenly icy audience that included Trecia. "It's an equivalent statement."

I smile back at Julie.

"Julia Roberts," I say.

Trecia starts growling.

Perhaps it is an accident of understanding on her part, a story my mother thinks she caught in Chinese, like a flu, from her parents. Why would she lie? She wouldn't lie; she doesn't. My mother is, when it suits her, honesty incarnate. Perhaps it is something Aunt Opal told her when she was a teenager. Or maybe she heard the story from a cousin in college. That is when I first heard the story, from my grandmother Ilene after I'd asked her what she thought of Po Po and Gung Gung when they all first met. By way of answering my question she told me the history of the laundromat, adding that my mother told it to her after my parents married.

I found out the story was a lie five years later, after calling Po Po to find out what the name of the Japanese neighbor was.

"What Japanese neighbor?" she asked.

"The one who sold the laundromat to Grandpa for a dollar."

"There was no Japanese neighbor who did that."

"Then how did Grandpa get the laundromat?"

"He bought it like anyone else! He bought it off Sam Wong because he was tired of driving a taxi."

I paused and tugged at the phone cord.

"There was no Japanese neighbor," I said slowly. "So there was no returned laundromat twenty years later?"

"No. Your grandfather kept the business and opened up another one by the Bon. In downtown."

I scratched large black circles into my notepaper with a pen.

"There was no Japanese neighbor," I said again.

"No! Your grandfather once hired a young Japanese kid to work for him, but he didn't get the laundry from him. Your grandfather didn't give him the laundry either."

"Well, what was *his* name?"

"Who knows! Who told you this?"

When I admitted it was my mother, Po Po laughed and said, "Your mother—" in such a knowing way I felt I should understand why Po Po would not finish this sentence.

When I called my parents to confirm whether it was actually my mother who had told the story, my father agreed. "Oh, yes," he said. "That was your mother's account of things." "Did you ever doubt it?" I asked. "Did you?" he demanded.

Later, my mother said it was what she had told him. It was what she'd heard. "Where?" I asked. "I can't really remember," she replied.

"Your father has a real dark side to him," Aunt Opal reportedly whispered to my mother once as a young woman, apropos, my mother insisted, of nothing. This phrase comes to me when I think of my mother's mistaken story (I will not call it a lie), and makes me wonder whether my mother half-remembered, half-assembled it as an attempt to display my grandfather's inherent goodness, erasing forever any possibility of evil percolating beneath his surface. Really, my mother never discovered what Opal meant by Gung Gung's having a dark side, just as I will never know how my mother came by the story of the laundromat, though I understand why so many people in the family—myself especially—want to believe it. It is almost too good to be true. It follows all the rules of multicultural mythology: a world war, a community rife with poverty and unspoken hatred, internment camps, even a laundromat! It touches upon two of the great themes in Asian-American culture—oppression and racial isolation—suggesting that some heroism and transcendence can be achieved; that, in fact, some transcendence was achieved by the farsightedness of my grandfather, who reportedly not only gave the laundry back for a dollar, but ran the other laundromat for years with the son of Y.

It is a story I have told Julie and Trecia during our vacation. They liked it, of course.

When I asked Po Po what she thought about my mother's story, however, she laughed.

"It never happened," she told me. "Nothing like that has ever happened to us."

The guidebook to the Philippines we have chosen is filled with useful and partially truthful information we choose to ignore. Only at moments of extreme boredom do we peruse "Culture," "History" and "Medical Information," all the sections typed in neat columns with boldfaced headings, little ink drawings ballooning alongside them of membranous shirts made from the threads of pineapple. Julie finds an article about a pseudo–Stone Age tribe the Philippine Ministry of Culture claimed to have found in 1971, called the Tasadays. *National Geographic* published a couple of articles and photographs of the twenty-six-member tribe in their leaf clothes, peacefully working around the cave they lived in. According to our guidebook, the hoax lasted for years since the government clamped down on outside access to the tribe. Thus the villagers hired to appear ingenuous before the world of Coke cans, steam engines, jeepneys and billboards lived on handouts from the government for almost a decade.

We are immediately fascinated. "Of course," Trecia says, "it would be easy to fool Americans." Julie glances at me but says nothing. We are on our way to buy plane tickets to Panay and neither of us wants to forgo the luxury of white sand beaches and cata-marans for the sake of an argument. Instead we agree with her as we wander the Manila airport searching for the right ticket office. Yes, of course, how could anyone believe such a story? But something in me balks, dismissing so quickly what seems to me to be our guidebook's cautionary tale. There must have been reasons, I think, for the creation of the Tasaday. There must have been enough evidence to make it believable.

Julie finds arrival and departure times written on a chalkboard by the domestic terminal. There is a crate of chickens in front of that and a group of Filipinos dozing on orange plastic benches as they wait for the ticket office to open at 2 A.M. "My flight leaves at three," says one kind but highly ineffectual gentleman. He tried to find us the phones (couldn't), tried to get us information on flights (couldn't), tried to direct a taxi driver to charge us by the meter. We ended up paying ten dollars for a two-minute ride.

"Are the planes to Panay full tomorrow morning?" we finally ask one man we find sitting behind a TRANSFER INFORMATION desk. He and four teenage boys lounging beside him riffle the contents of a desk drawer. "There are flights to Cebú. Are you going to Cebú?" he asks.

"No."

"That's too bad. Cebú is nice. Nice for people like you. You are going to Cebú?"

"No, we are going to Panay."

"Well, there is nothing there. Why do you want to go to Panay?"

Julie and I mutter something about being interested in beaches. The guard smiles. "That's nice," he says. "Go to Cebú."

"All the tourists are there," adds a teenager to our left.

"But are there flights to Panay?"

"There are no flights to Panay."

"Ever? Or just tomorrow?"

"Oh, no, there are flights. Every Tuesday and Thursday."

"But there are no flights *tomorrow?*"

"Oh, no, tomorrow is Tuesday."

"But you said there were no flights."

"Yes, there are no flights today."

"But we want one tomorrow!"

"Yes, you can go. There are flights tomorrow."

"When? The morning?"

"Whenever!" the man says, pointing to the schedule as if we hadn't paid the least attention to him. The teenage boys start joking to one another in Tagalog, eyeing Trecia's dark, straight hair, her nutmeg skin.

"I'm not Filipino," she says when the guard and the two boys try joking with her. Julie glances at her. Ah! her expression reads. Trecia sees it and shoots me a look I can't read because I'm trying to decipher whether I look Filipino, too, to them, to Julie, who tilts her head suddenly while eyeing my profile. "People think I'm every race alive," Trecia says pointedly to Julie and me. At this the guard and four teenagers laugh harder. Trecia shakes her head as she turns away but, from the slightly hostile expression on the men's faces as they watch us leave, I wonder if they think she's lying.

After a few minutes we go outside to sit and wait with the other Filipinos on the chairs. We watch the black night sky fade into a soft milky white, the night sounds thick around us. Far away are wild jungles, we know from reading the guidebook, rice paddies layered in giant steps like scallops of green lace on a woman's petticoat. I think about the Tasaday tribe snuggled in their cave just a few hundred miles from this airport. They shimmer into possibility, quickly dissolve. Nothing about them has ever existed. We won't see them, I know, stranded on my orange plastic desert island. I sleep as we wait for our flight.

"Asians have a lot of tests," my mother hesitantly told me when I asked what her friends thought when she married my white father. Was that the reason she created the story about Gung Gung's laundromat? But my mother isn't convinced this story is *not* true. "Po Po," my mother began, "is sometimes ashamed to admit the truth. It makes her seem less American."

Po Po is indeed astounded at our curiosity about her life and her husband's life, which she insists was boring, uneventful, American to the core. Perhaps Po Po's life was boring. It's certainly not so interesting to her now, with her children grown and her fingers zippered together with arthritis so that she can no longer knit. She hates to read, won't listen to music, despises animals. So it's the TV now, and visits from her grandchildren and church members, telephone calls, a few dinners out. No gambling. She tells me the races shouldn't mix when I call to ask about a cousin's getting married, his bride a Latina woman he met at work.

I try to picture how my mother came across the story of the laundromat. Was it something deliberate, to fool her husband and mother-in-law? I imagine her at age six or so, hiding under a cave-like table somewhere in the house, the one they used to live in on Jackson Street, white with hallways that stretch uninterrupted by wall or window from front porch to back porch. They have a dog that likes to lie under trucks and smell the gas fumes, the way my mother lies under her bed or a table breathing in the dust and crumbs of old food maybe, listening to her parents arguing in Chinese. It's something I used to do as a child, hiding under the piano bench or the small white shutter-door cabinet Gung Gung made for my bedroom. I didn't hide because my parents fought, but because I liked the sensation of being hidden, nestled away under protective shells of wood, corduroy, linen, the cold metal smell of the piano pedals or the biting fumes of mothballs around me. They were places that had distinct borders, understandable limits. I could pretend anything was true about me and my family and still feel safe. But they were always obvious places I chose; it surprised me when my parents couldn't find them. It would take very little imagination to uncover where I hid, I thought, listening to my parents as they called my name, as their feet pounded up and down the stairs. Now I suspect my parents knew exactly where I was but were simply keeping quiet about it. It was what they knew they were supposed to do: play along, say my name, pretend not to know where I was hiding.

The flight to Panay goes so badly we are afraid we will be killed in a crash. The plane's white sides rattle and heave as if the plane were vomiting, then the nose of the craft veers sharply toward a row of shanty houses built along the runway. Landing an hour and a half later, the plane repeats the violent shaking motions, its wheels smacking the runway so that we momentarily leave the ground again and bounce down the tarmac. Women clutch purses to them like life jackets. They pray with their eyes screwed shut against the oyster-colored sky that looms outside each bread loaf–sized window.

An hour's pause for lunch, then a bus ride for another five hours across the island. On our way to the Borocay boat terminal, Julie, Trecia and I bounce and slam into one another's sides on the bus. After our third hour riding, we reach hilly mud that the driver takes at 50 miles per hour, so that the bus lurches and heaves up slick brown crests of dirt only to be slapped down again with such violence we are all sure a tire will burst from the impact. The three of us sit in the very back of the bus, Trecia behind a young Filipino leaning out the window desperately trying to stop vomiting. I am behind a color TV perched on a sack of watermelons. At every turn the watermelons stampede in the direction of the most violent lurch, taking the TV along for the ride. The two friendly Filipino soldiers whom I am sitting with make halfhearted grabs for the TV as it dances by, groaning in its new plastic, but quit after a time and start smoking cigarettes.

Trecia is nauseous and can't talk. Tears stream down my face from all the dust in my eyes. Only Julie seems vaguely content, perched in between the two of us, but her black hair is stiff and thick with dirt, pasted in a black bush behind her like the Bride of Frankenstein's. The bus suddenly digs its back wheels into the dirt like a pit pony and we're at our first stop. The air is heavy with moisture, damp, skinlike. The soldiers beside me teach me a little Tagalog. We relax and eat coconut cakes bought from a vendor who appears on the bus, then settle back down as, with a sickening lurch, the bus snarls to life and bounds back along the road.

Outside our window the jungle seems to boil, a stew of palm leaves and grasses from which houses occasionally bob to the surface, along with people, thin shacks on stilts. The whole landscape appears to shift and change. It is easy to imagine things disappearing here, I think, and picture the Tasaday tribe living just out of the range of my vision, just past the curtain of trees beside the road.

The bus ride ends in a small town paved with dirt and sleeping dogs. We stumble off the bus to stretch before our last leg of the journey: another jeepney ride several miles to the port. But because the trip has been so exhausting, Julie convinces us to stop a little longer and photograph a nearby series of waterfalls our guidebook proclaims amazing. Initially none of us minds the hike, though as the road keeps curving on and on and we see no sign of our destination, we begin to feel the whole project is hopeless. Our week-long vacation is slipping away. All we've done is argue and travel for the past two and a half days on the most ludicrous and uncomfortable methods available: tricycles, jeepneys, back-road buses. "What's next, skateboards?" Julie mutters.

"At least we can say we saw the Philippines," I say. "Five minutes for each place."

Julie uses the guidebook to swat flies beside her.

"How much do you want to bet that guidebook was written by a white person," Trecia says.

"What does that mean?" Julie asks.

"Nothing that is described as beautiful is beautiful here," Trecia replies. "The restaurants suck, the accommodations are worse. God knows about the waterfall. The book is filled with all that tourist double-talk. The only reason anyone would recommend these things is if he thinks they are exotic."

"Then it's because he's gullible, not white," Julie says tightly.

"That's true," I add. "Julie's white and she doesn't find anything exotic."

Julie looks at me. "You are not helpful," she says.

We hail a tricycle driver and make it to the waterfall entrance. There, the guard insists we must pay an extra fare because the park is closing. It's almost five; no one else is nearby for miles. We pay and find, when we enter the park, a series of gray interconnected pools each about the depth and width of a child's bathtub, laddering down a small hill. Water sloshes thinly down, pool to pool, thick with a scum of cigarette butts, cola cans, Styrofoam cups. The three of us try laughing, but Julie's face blushes deep red.

After a long hike back to the main road, we soon find ourselves in a yelling match with another tricycle driver who insists a five-minute ride will cost us the equivalent of ten American dollars. It is dusk, we are missing the last ferry at the terminal, and Julie and the driver will not budge from their positions.

"Fifty pesos," the man insists. "It's a long way."

"It's only ten minutes from here; the woman in that store told us!" Julie shouts.

The man shrugs and looks away. Trecia and I beckon for other tricycle drivers. But Julie begins jerking her shoulders and making abrupt, chickenlike motions with her head. "Ever since we arrived here," she begins, "we have been overcharged and lied to. Now you are trying to rip us off!" The cabdriver stares at her as if she is touched. Trecia and I drift off to admire, and hide behind, the shrubbery. "You should not cheat visitors!" Julie yells again, her shoulders shaking. Then, unbelievably, she snarls, "You do *not represent your country well!*"

"Well," I say to Julie as the tricycle driver peels out of the shallow ditch and back onto the road. "We missed that ferry."

"In Austria," Julie continues, "if you have a bad time and tell the people there you had a bad time, they are genuinely concerned. They ask you what happened, where it happened, and how it happened and then they *apologize.* They are truly upset if a visitor has a bad time in their country!"

Trecia stares at her for a long moment. "That's nice," she finally says.

A deep belching from down the road alerts us to the approach of a jeepney, luggage rolling along the hood under its flimsy rope ties, chicken feathers streaming from its back like wedding confetti. People are packed into every crevice, we see, from every angle, and every one of them looks deeply, irrevocably miserable.

"This is definitely our ride," I tell Julie, who laughs until she starts to hiccup. She calms down for a while, bursts out laughing again, leaning against me as I haul her into the jeepney. Trecia and I give her a look when we see she can't stop giggling, and Julie blushes again. "It's just so hard in Asia," she starts to say, or I think she starts to say, but then she's doubled up once more and, when we sit down among the other women it looks, almost, as if she's crying.

Julie follows me through Borocay's various market stalls filled with wooden rice gods, tie-dyed dresses, gold-plated bangles on strings. Neither of us is interested in buying anything; we simply want to walk.

"I have to say," Julie tells me as she follows me into a stall of jewelry, "that I'm tired of you siding with Trecia. You both gang up on me and it's not fair."

"That's not true," I tell her.

"Don't lie," she replies. "You do."

I look at the freckles dotting the papery bridge of her nose. They have been appearing over the past few days in the sun slowly, one by one, like lemon juice stains scorched under lamplight. Now they are amoeba-shaped, broken hearts.

"OK," I tell her. "I do."

"I feel like I'm supposed to be ashamed of something, as if things were easy for me or there was a way I should behave that is different from you. But I don't know what that way is. I feel like you and Trecia are making up these rules as we go along."

"You're right, it isn't fair," I tell her. I touch a blue skirt, dangle the fringe between my fingers.

"Well," she says.

"Well," I repeat.

"I wish you would tell Trecia."

"I don't think she'll agree."

"Probably not," she says.

I leave Julie when we reach the beach. I hand her the guide-book and the sunscreen, the blankets and the journals. I swim out into the pale blue water ringed with unexpected algae, a scum of green frills that stick to my swimsuit and thighs. Trecia can't stand the sun and is asleep with a headache in the bungalow we've rented; Julie, on the beach, has covered her face with a book. I float in the warm Pacific, just as I planned to float, my fingers turn-ing to shrimp in the brine. I turn my head and watch Julie's long white form get swallowed by the sand as I bob by, growing slim, growing fine, disappearing.

The Tasaday tribe was found in the late 1960s on Mindanao Island, southeast of Panay and Luzon, the main island, where Manila is located. They were found living without metal tools, agriculture, cloth, speaking a language unknown and entirely dis-tinct from those of the other nearby villagers. They were, accord-ing to the report, a three-hour walk to the nearest village, which evidently they never took, preferring to hide instead deep in the forest as if they suspected what horrors they would find if they left. For thousands of years the tribe never wandered far from the cave in which they were found, the rules of their own civilization. These facts I heard about from Julie who reread the history section in the guidebook. A few hours after our talk, she insisted that I read it again as well. When I found the book nestled in my backpack, I picked it up to investigate. The story had been outlined for me to read, with notes, in blue.

According to the guidebook, what captured the public's imag-ination was the Tasaday tribe's peaceful—almost utopian—exis-tence. In all the Tasadays' history there had been no killings, no wars, no sexual discrimination. The Tasaday purportedly lived free from violence or cruelty, treating their women equally and apparently without jealousy: the tribe practiced a form of Stone Age free love.

This, at least, was the story told to the West by the Philippine Ministry of Culture. And who could really deny it, lacking access to the tribe? There were skeptics, but the popular ideal of the utopian Tasaday remained ideal to the West largely because of a lack of information and the attractiveness of its myth. A book by John Nance entitled *The Gentle Tasaday* was eventually published, in which the Tasaday were praised for their message of peace and cultural harmony. It was a Swiss journalist named Oswald Iten who finally discovered the truth. Upon finding their cave empty when he went to visit them, Iten discovered the Tasaday living with other villagers in the surrounding area, wearing T-shirts and drinking Cokes, speaking Tagalog, having lived for years on rice handouts from the government minister blamed for orchestrating the hoax.

But the strangest information I found out about the Tasaday was that, in 1989, the American Anthropological Association published a book by the anthropologist Thomas Headland in which it was concluded that the Tasaday did *not* deliberately deceive the public. They couldn't have, since the Tasaday, Headland claimed, hadn't thought up the idea themselves. Perhaps the government was at fault for concocting the story, but if such poor efforts were made to conceal the truth, can we really call the culture minister the culprit? Nor are there clear reasons for the lie—how would tourism have flourished if the government refused to let people see the Tasaday?—and so the hoax itself seems more like a curious oversight than a deliberate attempt to swindle, a ridiculous mistake.

Julie, I can see from her notations on the Tasaday in the guidebook, wants to show me how artificial and voluntary—even malicious—definitions about "otherness" are. The Tasaday never existed—we wanted them to exist. Likewise, her reasoning tacitly continues, perhaps my point of view and loyalties in Asia are not inherently so different from her own. But, as Julie insinuates in dark blue circles and check marks throughout the guidebook's history section, I cannot accept that. I need myths and stories and fables. I need to create an identity that will satisfy my ideas about what it means to be half Chinese, hiding or obliterating what personal traits do not uphold this image. Just as Americans and Europeans in the late 1960s needed the Tasaday to define, in part, what they expected Asia to be. Gentle savages. Primitive utopians.

This is what interests me about the Tasaday hoax: the audience that believed it. Reading this story in the guidebook, I cannot help but feel that the West's positive reception to the Tasaday was based on racism, a deep-seated belief in the inferiority of the Philippines. But then, thinking of my mother's story about the laundromat, which on the surface also seems to have been a hoax, I wonder whether that racist condescension actually ran the other way. Perhaps the Philippine minister of culture assumed he could get away with it, believing that the West was gullible when it came to Asia. Perhaps he thought he understood what the West was already willing to believe.

Again, I am brought back to my grandfather's mysterious acquisition of the laundromat. When I think about my mother's story about Gung Gung, I do not think of Po Po or any of my mother's brothers, but my white friends' faces, nodding in appreciation. None of my other Chinese relatives know this story. I think of my mother embellishing—perhaps lying about—her father's heroism as a means of impressing herself and perhaps an audience unfamiliar with what it would mean to be Asian-American. The story has its requisite exotic, historical moments. It is certainly not like the stories of my white friends' grandparents during World

War II. And yet it also offers us the idea of hope—in the unlikely and peaceable alliance of impoverished strangers, our ethnic under-dogs triumphing against a racist society—that seems to me to be something straight out of Hollywood. It tells us that ethnicities in America can and should befriend one another, can and should dis-appear into an assimilated utopia that won't worry the dominant culture. But the story ultimately lacks the unresolved grittiness—the dark side—of what it means for immigrant cultures to attempt or to achieve this assimilation. My Chinese grandfather and Y. are larger-than-life characters who remain, tantalizingly, faceless: the Everymans of Asian-America. Like the Tasadays' peace-loving society (how apropos a discovery for the hippies in the Vietnam era! And how believable this lack of civilization might be in Asia!), perhaps my mother's story about these men and their laundromat was one that white Americans needed to hear. Perhaps by telling this story my mother (sick of being the one dark spot in a sea of paler faces?) could make *herself* seen by this audience. She could make herself visible.

And I, evidently, am not so different from her. I also remember how exciting the story was to me when I first heard it. It made sense viscerally. But the history of the laundromat was not, of course, Po Po's version of history or Gung Gung's version of his-tory, or even the history of any of my young Chinese cousins who have never heard about this laundromat. It is my version. My mother's story has evolved into the story of her white husband and mother-in-law and daughter. Like the Tasaday hoax, it's what we—the outsiders—want to believe happened. It's what I want to think about when I think about my Asian family in America, just as Trecia and I want to believe there are certain things that include us inherently in our mothers' cultures. In this Julie is right—if there weren't easily recognizable rules for being Asian, Trecia and I would invent them as we went along. Because being Asian in

America is a fact that does and does not exist. It disappears from view when scrutinized directly, like certain stars or planets at night, only to resurface in unexplainable tastes or angers or prejudices that roll in on tidal shifts, the irregular tug of the moon. We need stories, unquestionable paradigms for behavior and history when everything else about us—our appearance, our language, our preferences—is in question. It is our own kind of defense. Growing up, we have always been aware of an audience that is prepared to define us. We know how these imposed definitions can cover us up, obliterate us. Like my mother's story or the Tasaday hoax, Trecia's draconian racial definitions, I understand, are at least *hers*.

"That never happened, nothing ever happened," Po Po insists to her family, hoping to negate herself.

She doesn't understand why we don't listen to her. She doesn't understand how, in cases like this, it's not the truth that always matters.

At Borocay—exhausted from two days' and seven hours' traveling—my friends and I find cheap, canned mango drinks at a restaurant facing the ocean, and a white sand beach. We slip off our sandals and roll up the sleeves of our T-shirts. We are truly enjoying ourselves for the first time since we arrived in the Philippines, and this fact is only heightened by the knowledge that, as Julie figured out this afternoon while discussing ferry schedules with a local guide, we have to leave at 6 A.M. the very next morning to make our flight back to Seoul.

Julie writes in the sand with a toe. Trecia dozes happily beside me. What should we do tonight but get drunk and watch the stars? I'll eat more than my fair share of the coconut shrimp we order and this time Trecia will only smile. Souvenirs, boys, the beach for less than twenty-four hours. The Pacific growls and purrs.

What will we tell our families when we return? "The truth," Trecia replies, watching the green water lap and lap the shore. "We had a good time."

If I have children I will tell them my mother's story about Gung Gung's laundromat. There are Chinese families, many of them in fact, who made these sorts of arrangements with Japanese families before the internment. There are Chinese families who would have done these exact things.

But I understand I will be telling them what my mother was like, what she thought her father was like, what I am like for wanting to believe it. I understand I will be laying out for them certain tropes of the Asian-American or immigrant experience so that when I tell them the true story, how my grandfather simply saved enough money to give up the taxi in favor of wet sheets and bluing, they will know just how much we do not really fit these images. Then, how much we do.

The real story behind how my grandfather acquired the laundromat is my mother. So this is it. In January 1945 my mother is barely a child, only five years old. It is Seattle, it rains all the time during winter, and my grandfather catches colds easily, slogging from home to the laundromat and its steamy interior. My mother grows up walking between home and Twenty-third street, the laundry where Gung Gung will sometimes give her enough money for a Wimpy's hamburger as an after-school treat. The neighborhood is different now—there are no pigeon sellers walking through the streets with their filthy cages, no ice carts her mother urges her to buy a brick of ice from. Her friends are Japanese, Chinese, one or two white girls. As she grows up, however, all the people around her seem different. What is she? Who is she? She meets my father.

But today it's raining and that hasn't happened. Instead she trots down the sidewalk with her rain hat askew, chubby legs spattered with mud. The sky is gray on gray, the sun a gloomy pearl above her. She turns the corner to the blare of car horns and puffs of exhaust, searching for the copper edge of pennies glinting from the cracks in the sidewalk. All the signs here are furious scrawls, blocky red and black and white characters she can't read but knows the meaning of anyway: not hers, not hers, not hers. Hers. She stops in front of the Lucky Laundromat.

There's my grandfather. Thin and overworked. My mother pushes open the door. Her father pats back the thin dark strings of his greased hair and steps in front of the counter to meet his next-to-youngest. My grandfather the taxi driver, the gambler, possessor of a dark side, the man my family assumes momentarily and incorrectly is murdered in a Vietnamese gambling hall in 1983. This man, the unknowable, smiles and reaches for her. Now he shuts the laundry and walks outside, my mother's hand stuffed in his hand for safety as he guides her home, looking both ways for traffic.

Biology

Today it's high school, and I'm slumped over a box or beaker of something that won't work. Beside me Paul Ling etches sarcastic notes onto our class project paper, drops his pen, flushes from the effort of all his weight suddenly piling on top of his head as he reaches down to grab it from the floor. The teacher has left and we are on our own. Our desks have been arranged in little helixes of four, a ring of science tables lacing the edges of the dim classroom. Has it been raining? The white blinds squint shut, the overhead fluorescent tubes flicker behind their metal grating, a filthy American flag furls in the breeze of someone's throwing something at a friend.

In this box (beaker?) we are working on something potentially genetic, which is great for Paul Ling, who has personally developed many genetic theories this year, about racial compatibility, about IQ. "That's not a good mix," he has already warned me about my own parentage: Norwegian, Chinese. At first I think he means it is a bad mix of physical features and squirm at the thought that he is calling me ugly, but soon realize he's just critiquing the combination of cuisines: "What do you *eat?*" he asks.

Paul himself eats well, all Chinese. He is fat, very tall, with broad features and short hair that sticks up in dark spindles and looks separated: charred cornstalks ruffled by the wind. Because he is fat he appears to have developed breasts about the size of my own, which is doubly unfortunate for him since his name already sounds feminine. "Pauliiiine," the boys in the back coo. Paul Ling is cynical, smart, lazy, speaks in an agonizing lisp. We do some problems in our biology book, fiddle with whatever I can't remember lies inside the box. Everyone gossips when the teacher leaves the room, so nothing gets done.

Suddenly to our right stands Mark Brown, the older brother of Gary, whom I have gone to school with all my life. Mark is a football player, a senior in a biology room full of sophomores who are all (unlike him) right on track for graduation with their science credits. He has black hair and brilliant eyes, skin that looks smoke-colored. He wears his green and gold football jersey today, the silken, web mesh that reminds me of frog skin shimmering in the fluorescence. His massive brows have worked together into a single hairy minus sign above his eyeballs. He stares at the two of us. It is rumored Mark Brown is popular, though we haven't seen much evidence of it. Like almost everyone I know, he's a satellite along the fringes of some crowd or other. "What?" Paul asks, tentatively trying out a testy lisp. He's had it with the Pauline thing.

"Ching chong chang," Mark Brown retorts. Paul and I look at each other. Mark smiles and repeats, louder, "Ching chong chang." He pulls back the dun skin around his eyes to mimic slants, but all I see are the red webs in the corners of his sockets, the thin skin grotesquely stretched over his bulging, glue-colored eyes. He has evolved into a gila monster. He continues to sing, turning his head to Paul and then to me, serenading.

Paul raises an eyebrow, glancing at me. *You want to say something here?* He yawns and I feel slightly left out. So I shrug and try to see us from the little keyhole of Mark's perspective: two flat-faced, unnaturally raisin-eyed students, one too fat, one too thin. Mark's face is red, but this might be from the contortions he's putting it through.

After another few seconds Mark retreats, bored by our lack of reaction. He keeps his eyes on us as he stalks off, however, his fingers stretching his eye skin out a little more insistently and his voice still humming the anthem. Softer, softer, it only dies when he realizes, finding his own table again, how weak the sound of his voice is in the classroom.

Traveling to Opal

Just outside Natchez, Mississippi, comes a storm of such torrential proportions I have to pull the car I've borrowed off the road. The storm bursts along the highway; to my right flash strings of lightning like neon veins that appear to pierce the trees just alongside the other lane of cars. Raindrops fall hard and close together; it is more like several bathtubs of water being poured over the road. There are ditches of runoff so deep in the concrete that when my car plows into them it sounds as if I were going through a car wash, the water jets on either side of me like brushes beating against the car's metal body. Other vehicles have slowed to an anxious creep, which I can't see until I am almost right behind the bumper of a truck, its taillights glowering hazily through a curtain of rain.

I pull off the road at the first gas station and wait inside the minimart with two older black men who have stopped for the same reason. They both wear white T-shirts spackled with grease over jeans or canvas work pants as faded and dirtied as their tops. The wrinkles in their hands have clay in the creases. They smoke and look at me sideways when I ask the cashier how far I am from a motel. "Just down the road about a half a mile, ma'am," she replies in the strongest accent I have ever heard. "Where you from?"

"Seattle," I reply. I have just moved to Atlanta, Georgia, with Joseph but have been coached by a friend from Louisiana not to say this. It would be impossible by any Southern standard for me to actually be from Atlanta, he argued. I'll stick out anyway. Better just be honest.

The cashier says nothing, though she continues to watch me. *What the hell are you doing here?* her look asks. I have no idea. I told Joseph I was investigating the history of Po Po's sister, Opal, who had lived in Natchez in the early part of the century with her husband, a Chinese grocer whom she divorced and ran away to Seattle to avoid. It's a vacation of sorts. Unfortunately, as Joseph pointed out, I'm already unemployed.

When I asked Po Po about Opal's divorce, she insisted that it was her brother-in-law's fault. "Opal asked him to send money back to her mother in China," she explained. "But he refused. He said our mother could just go die instead!"

She told me this over the phone the morning after I had finished my shift on the hotline for the Women's Resource Center, a battered women's clinic. Six hours listening to strangers weep on the phone. "I need help," one woman whispered. "My boyfriend just hung my cat. He left her dangling in the bathroom so I'd find her when I got home."

"And?" I asked Po Po, sighing into the mouthpiece.

"Isn't that enough?" she'd asked.

My great-aunt Opal died four years ago. There's not much left to her life except this story and a videotape my mother made while interviewing her for a Chinese history project. On the tape you can see Opal wearing an oatmeal-colored sweater with little sheep knitted around the collar. She sits in a leather easy chair, and her small feet, sheathed in Keds, dangle just above the ground. Her skin, poreless, taut and fine, looks gray-tinged on the screen. Her eyes behind her glasses are blue from glaucoma. Planes occasionally roar overhead, a huge metallic rushing that floods the tape. My mother is asking Opal about her childhood, the names of her brothers and sister. "Clear Snow, Plum Blossom, Jade Heart." "Pretty names," my mother says. "Pretty names," Opal grimaces. "Not pretty people." She's happy on the tape, being asked to tell what irritates her sister Po Po to hear; in just a few more minutes she'll spill everything. Over the tape Opal brings up tongs, so-and-so's alcoholism, the Chinese immigrant women who killed themselves in lockup. "So sad," she says. "So sad." A plane shrieks in the background.

Now Opal's favorite story: her father, the head of a tong, receives death threats from a rival. He goes back to Hong Kong after breaking up his family in Seattle and sending his girls to such far reaches as New York and Canton to be cared for by relatives. Once in Hong Kong, however, he dies of the sickness that had been gnawing at him for half a decade. After his death, his brother tells Opal's mother he won't give her money for the funeral unless she gives him her last plot of land: the only resource she has to live on. She's stuck: she followed the wrong man; now she's succumbing to the wrong advice.

"My father gave his brother everything, a chance in America, everything," Opal drones. "But he was lazy, and a bad doctor, too. He made his fortune boiling mulberry leaves, then drying them up and selling them as medicine."

"What did it cure?" My mother's voice.

"Everything, supposedly."

The Natchez Trace is a trail cutting northeast from Natchez to Tennessee. Animals first created the path, then Native Americans followed it; pioneers, traders and mail carriers later widening its swath as they traveled back and forth from Mississippi. Earlier this afternoon, driving down the Trace alone, I found masses of kudzu sprouting there, devoured by the viny green plant. Through the rain they took on shapes of animals or giants clutching objects fiercely to them: a hammer, a suitcase, a baby. Heat radiated from the road in clouds of steam, water misting off blacktop.

It seemed lush, tropical, the heat as sensual as another body wrapped around me whenever I exited the car. I can't picture Opal here, small-boned, precise Opal lost in the overgrowth, the violent conflagration of weeds with weeds, tree branches tangling into one another. "Call me as soon as you get there," my boyfriend warned. He won't admit it, but he's sure something bad will happen to me. I'll get killed or hurt; I'll run away with his car, leaving him and my half a year's unpaid rent to manage. This is my favorite story: I think of Opal asking me, when I was twelve years old, about my future. How many children did I want when I grew up? "I could have a child, I guess," I mused. "But then I couldn't get married. I don't think I could take care of two people."

At the gas station minimart, more people enter, dripping wet from the walk here out of their cars, shivering in the blast of air-conditioning. A young black man buys a Slim Jim and a Coke, I eat a bag of uranium-colored Doritos, a middle-aged blonde rifles through the candy bars. We stand at odd angles and eye one another and (is it my imagination?) it seems more than a few looks get shot at me, the foreigner. I clearly don't belong here with my accent and outfit. I am dressed like a fashionable college student: khaki shorts, slip-on sandals, navy and pink stretch T-shirt. The men are in overalls and torn cotton shirts, the women in sweatpants. When the storm clears enough I go back outside to my car and drive on, though the rain soon comes down as hard or even harder than before and I am forced to stop again. For the next hour I make my way like this: starting up when the rain dies, parking on the side of the road when it doesn't. I curse myself for impatience each time I stop, but I can't stand sitting in an unmoving car. My hands shake and I sweat hearing trucks rumble by, too close. I turn the key in the ignition and wipe down the steamy insides of the windows with my forearm. Rain hits the car roof like tossed stones. From the passenger window loom more trees, engorged with kudzu. I start the car and drive.

My friend Rob warned me about Mississippi. He went to college in New Orleans, refers to himself as one of "the dirt-eating poor." In e-mails, he sent me slightly hysterical, cryptic messages about the dangers I would face. Don't go alone, he wrote. Don't fake a southern accent or leave the beaten path. You have never been anywhere like this before.

Just how rural is this place? I wrote back, to which he replied, You'll see when you get there.

Concerned, I spoke with another southern friend, Dana. "Is there something southerners know about Mississippi that northerners don't?" I asked. We were at a Moroccan restaurant, sitting on two garish stuffed cushions. I watched Dana shake her napkin out delicately onto her lap. She is a native Atlantan whom I would seriously hesitate to swear in front of. She is also the kind of woman who manages to have perpetually well-applied lipstick.

"No," she replied slowly. "There's nothing wrong with Mississippi. I don't know what your friend was telling you that for. I mean, it's not as if you're *black*."

Our waiter, who was black, raised an eyebrow from his corner station.

"So there's no problem driving there by myself?"

"Oh, no."

"And there's no problem with my accent?"

"It's OK. You aren't a *Yankee*. No, you're somewhere in between. People won't know what to do with you. Where is your friend from?"

"Louisiana."

"Oh, my," she said. "Now *there* is a state."

I thought briefly about asking some of the other women I worked with at the Center what they thought about Mississippi, the South, as a way of making small talk. But trivial conversation seems somehow wrong. "He never used to be like this," a woman told me yesterday at the legal clinic, her eye purpled in red and blue-black crescents beneath the lid. "He calls my work now every ten minutes. He threw me into a wall and hit my chest with a small desk safe."

What's the worst that could really happen to me? I wrote Rob.

Enough, he replied.

In Natchez, I sleep at the first motel I find, at the very edge of town. In the morning I drive into downtown, past crumbling homes and pink bushes, my purse loaded with the free maps the desk clerk has given me. Natchez is a tourist town. At the time of the Civil War it was home to more millionaires per capita than any other city in the United States; because of its wealth, Natchez was used as one of the Union's headquarters during the war, which saved its antebellum homes. Yellow fever from mosquitoes that bred on the banks of the Mississippi wiped out children and young mothers. Now there is a riverboat gambling casino and enough pollution to protect everyone. Now there are fancy hotels, Confederate-themed dinners and dances. No Chinese.

For the second time this morning I nearly turn the car around and drive back home. There is nothing here, I can see already, flipping through pamphlets filled with visions of hoop skirts and balustrades. I'm embarrassed to go in search of Opal, the Mississippi Chinese, simply because the idea of it intrigues me.

But when I get to the Visitors' Center on Canal Street I change my mind again and stop. A blast of air-conditioning hits me as I clear the doors, and my entire body goes limp; the car I've borrowed doesn't have air-conditioning and it is 95 degrees outside excluding humidity. I walk into the lobby of the Center and find an information computer kiosk that plays, oddly, the theme from *Gone With the Wind*. In the room off to its right is an enormous panorama of an 1850s drawing of the Natchez area printed onto a wall-sized poster that scrolls slowly. As I watch, a scene of an Indian tribe scalping several white settlers comes into view.

Crowds of older couples swirl around me, a blur of pastel plaid Bermudas and polo shirts. I collect new maps, sidle up to the information desk to ask an older woman about some sites around town and then, hesitantly, whether there has ever been a Chinese community. The woman blinks at me for several seconds. She has on bright red lipstick that has begun to fade orange around the edges of her mouth. "A Chinese community?" she asks.

"Yes," I say, feeling stupid.

"In Natchez?"

I nod.

She keeps staring. "No, ma'am," she says finally. "There's just us. Just Natchez," she says. "Everyone—blacks, white, Chinese, we're all in here together."

"So there's no area where the Chinese live. Historically, I mean?"

"No, ma'am."

I thank her, blushing, and walk off. It is difficult for me to interpret her remark: does she mean Natchez was simply too small to have distinct communities, or that Natchez is not—has not ever been—segregated by the virtue of being free-thinking, liberal Natchez? I leave the Center and get sucked up like a crumb into a vacuum of scorching air. My back skin sears into the seat as I fiddle with the broken fan dials in the car. I give up and leave the car at the Visitors' Center. "We're all in here together," I mutter to myself as I begin my slow walk in the intense heat around town. After five minutes, my feet have begun to drag from the weight of my sandals. A man honks from a pickup truck, waves and slows down. "Need a ride?" he calls. I shake my head with all the strength I have left, and he shoots away, all air-conditioning, neighborly concern and country music. I see him glance back at me curiously in his rearview mirror.

Up Canal Street, I turn into a garden that boasts huge bursts of pink and yellow flowers outside Rosalie Mansion and what might possibly be a gazebo, now the loveliest word in the English language. Sweat puckers along my forearms and around the back of my dress. To my relief I find a sign on the mansion's black iron gates declaring that tours are held every half hour through the air-conditioned home. I hurry to buy a ticket.

The woman who leads me on my solo tour recites her facts in a slightly panicked voice. She has blond hair and a sweat-free brow and, at the end of the tour, stares at my chest with an expectant look. She has been staring at my chest off and on for the full half hour and I am beginning to realize that my outfit might not be appropriate. I am wearing a scoop-necked blue sleeveless dress that falls to just above the knees because if I wear anything more I am going to die. The blond guide stares at the crescent of skin above my neckline. That driver probably wasn't being neighborly. "Any questions?" the tour guide asks my breasts.

"Actually," I say, folding my arms, "are there any Chinese in Natchez?"

"What?" Her eyes flicker toward mine in surprise.

"Chinese."

She thinks for a minute. "No, ma'am," she says at last. "Though we had some Chinese when I was in school. Actually, we had one Chinese. But there were two Chinese in my grade school. Girls. They were the Lees."

"So you grew up here?"

"Yes, ma'am. I'm a native Nah-cheesian."

"Excuse me?"

"I grew up in Natchez. There's a professor at Alcorn, Dr. Lee, who is the girls' father but he's hard to understand. Actually, they're all hard to understand."

"So they aren't native . . . Natchezians?"

"No, ma'am."

We look out the white porch of Rosalie onto the street. To our far right I can just make out two stands of trees that bridge a widening of the Mississippi. Brown river, blue sky.

"There *was* a large Jewish community here," the tour guide adds helpfully as she leads me out. "Bankers for the rich."

"What happened to them?" I ask.

"They left," she replies. She nods politely as the broad screen door swings shut behind me.

My mother told me she didn't know her aunt Opal had been married twice until Opal's eldest children arrived to join her and her new family in Seattle from where they'd been staying with relatives in Texas. Po Po said they were from Opal's "southern marriage."

"I don't think she talked about it because he wasn't a very good husband," my mother said.

I wonder whether this is a euphemism. Does it mean he came home late, was irresponsible with money, drank, slept around? Was he violent? My boyfriend and I slid Opal's video in the VCR and watched Opal's tiny face ripple through the grainy television weave. When my mother got to the part about Opal's time in Mississippi, Opal's mouth clamped tight. "Oh," she said, her words slurring a bit in that strange accent of hers, part drawl, part clipped northern speech. "That's a *long* story."

I think about Opal at the Women's Resource Center occasionally. There's a woman I walked through a protective order at the courthouse whose boyfriend just moved her to Georgia to be with him. He gets drunk and trashes her apartment, burns her carpet, breaks her collection of glass figurines whenever she threatens to leave him. When she tried to call the police last time he grabbed her around the throat, his big fist loosening and tightening to keep her always on this side of consciousness. This is not something I can picture happening to Opal.

The thumbnail history of the Chinese in Mississippi I learn in Natchez's elegant, square public library, a stone's throw from the town's one synagogue (not all the Jews left, apparently), three blocks from the tiny depot. I flip through books on Natchez history nestled between works like *Redneck Heaven*, *The South Was Right*, *Southern by the Grace of God*. None of these look as if they'd ever been checked out.

Flipping through *Along the Trace*, I learn that after the Civil War, planters seeking cheap labor to replace slaves recruited workers from Italy, eastern Europe and China. One plantation called Welham even named a section of its property the Chinese Quarters because of all the Chinese housed there to help with sugar production. But according to the book, the planters disliked Chinese workers. They made bad slaves, one owner said. Too small-boned, too slow to pick up the language. That, and the fact that they kept fainting in the heat.

From what little I know, Opal's husband was not born near the Trace, no child of sugar slaves. Instead he was like the other Chinese grocers here: Cantonese, Baptist, probably a resident in one of the poorer white or all-black communities. From two short sociology books the reference librarian digs out for me, I learn he could have married black here though he obviously didn't; could not have educated his children in the white schools though he could at the black ones (almost no Chinese did this, preferring home tutoring), and, most surprisingly, probably believed he would never stay. We were simply passing through, Chinese told researchers who asked. Only after decades passed and they and their children still had not gone did they realize they were stuck. Actively or not, they had chosen to remain.

I take down notes, skim pages. For a Monday afternoon the library is surprisingly busy. Groups of schoolchildren and frustrated-looking teachers pop up around the stacks, chase each other through hallways. The reference librarian at his desk helps a gentleman also searching for the history of his family, and I read under the watchful eye of several young black boys who camp out in nearby chairs to read, occasionally putting down their books to look around them hopefully, as if something will be more interesting.

Around me flow the rising and falling of the women's accents, higher-pitched, more feminine than what I am used to. Only the irritated librarian sounds shrill as she runs around a cluster of children telling them to stop touching things on people's desks. She doesn't seem to like her job; when I ask her if she knows of any other books on Chinese history in Mississippi she snaps,

"That's a job for the reference desk," and flicks her wrist at the man who has been helping me. Later when I ask for a receipt for my photocopies she narrows her eyes at my chest and sighs, a little dramatically.

"Where you from?" she asks my breasts aggressively.

"Seattle."

She says nothing. But when I scoop up my change she tilts her head and fixes me with a sidelong, penetrating look, an expression I can't read.

Outside the library, heat clubs me nearly motionless. I practically have to crawl toward the commercial section of town, nodding back at the few older men who smile at me, one or two of them tipping their hats. While the men seem friendly, the women appear slightly hostile, neither smiling nor nodding, offering up only so much information as is necessary. Is it my dress? I get turned around, ask a man for directions and end up learning where I must have lunch, dinner, what the best recent movie is and the weather for the week. Women waft by, coifed, powdered, icy creatures of the indoors. I sweat shamelessly in the street.

Is this what Opal felt like? I try to picture her here, in the violet-colored evenings, her face filmed with powder, wearing a dress the color of her name. All the women parade outside the store, white on white, looking in only when they have to buy something.

That's when I turn another block and pass a window in which I see my first evidence: a middle-aged man with glasses in a suit and tie, laughing. His hair is white around the temples, he is deeply tanned with lines cut into his face like shiny rivulets. He looks distinctly Chinese. I stop and try not to stare, walk on a little ways, then come back as if I'm searching for an address so that I can get another look. The man sees me, stops laughing and raises his eyebrows. I start walking away, but then another man in a navy suit comes hurrying out to ask if I need help. "Are you looking for someone, ma'am?" he asks. I freeze, seeing the sign behind him announcing that the building is a law firm.

"Someone, something else was here," I babble. I don't want to go in and ask this stranger what he knows about Chinese in Natchez. I picture myself through his eyes—some sticky, under-dressed girl from the North with too many tourist brochures—and see, suddenly, how strange a request this is. It is too private a question. What right do I have to do this research? What right do I have to ask this man to spill his history and ethnic affiliations, to call attention—no matter how nicely—to his race?

The lawyer smiles at me. He offers to help me find what I am looking for, calling out street names and law firm addresses in a friendly but insistent voice. I shake my head instead and hurry away, trying not to seem like I was spying in his window.

City Hall keeps no records of its past citizens. This I learn at three, in the small room off to the right of the clean marble foyer. The rooms all seem to be made of dark maple, and each door has above it a stiffly numbered sign on a plastic tag. For a moment it feels as if I've stepped into the 1950s. When I reach the records room, the brunet secretary there advises me to go to the Historic Natchez Foundation only after some flustered thought. "Chinese?" she asks. "In Natchez? I don't. . . . Ma'am, I don't think I've ever heard anything like that in all my life."

She has, however, heard of a certain photography collection of all Natchez. I am soon given the number for a Dr. Sanders, who bought negatives from some portrait artists who recently passed away. In the collection he might have one or two pictures of Chinese. Street scenes, perhaps, or a portrait. She is doubtful, but I am desperate so I call.

"Are you Chinese?" is the first thing he asks when I tell him what I'm looking for. I smile. I am sure this is what the other people I have questioned in person have also been privately wondering.

"Half," I tell him.

"Half, huh? We used to call those kind Eurasians in Tsingtao. I used to work there as a doctor a long time ago when I was in the Navy. And when I was a child in a small town in Louisiana, I remember seeing a Chinese man married to a black woman, though I don't remember if they had children. I don't think there were any Chinese in Natchez, however. I don't think there was any such community here."

Having said this, however, Dr. Sanders clearly feels some responsibility to give me any information he can about the Chinese, about China. This is a common response. The most common response, of course, is the quizzical stare accompanied by silence, though Chinese free-association runs a close second. "I like Chinese food," said one museum clerk. "There's the Hunan restaurant on 61. It's got a great buffet. If you like that sort of thing."

"Segregation made Chinese kids go to white schools in Louisiana," Dr. Sanders tells me now, to which I grunt softly in surprise. This contradicts my reading. "Did you know that?" he continues. "And did you know that Chinese citizens could enroll in the U.S. Navy? Did you?"

"No, sir," I reply.

"I made house calls into the native households in China. I have dug mustard plaster off so many little Chinese babies. You ever hear of that? They would paint it on thickly."

"How did you become interested in China?" I ask.

"Oh, Pearl S. Buck. You ever hear of her? I used to read everything she published. Just fascinated me. I always thought it would be wonderful to go. I just loved the people. I was crazy about Chinese!"

"Have you gone back?" I ask.

"I haven't," he replies. "I have such an aversion to Communism. But not to the Chinese."

Before I say good-bye, Dr. Sanders remembers something else, a photo of a woman he could never place. "She was black, maybe, or Chinese," he says. "You know, sometimes a lot of blacks look Asian. You could take a look at the photo. I gave it to the African-American museum that is at the old post office? It's closed but people say you can walk right in."

So I hike to the museum and find it, as Dr. Sanders said, easily opened. Plaster and a soft dust of old stripped paint lies everywhere; ladders and bits of paraphernalia are stacked around the rooms. There are no pictures.

Frustrated and yet fascinated by the idea of this half-black, half-Chinese woman's portrait, I go back to the museum of historic photographs of Natchez to have a look. And, maybe it is Dr. Sander's description, maybe it is my own preoccupation with the Chinese, but almost everyone begins to look Asian. One woman in particular, her hair drawn back tight against her scalp, has the dark, lidless eyes of an Asian girl. I stand and stare at this portrait for over a minute, watching this woman grow more and less Chinese. She reminds me of David Carradine. As a child I'd been a devoted fan of *Kung Fu* and had grown up thinking that Carradine really was Chinese. When I told my mother this a few years ago she shook her head and said that she should have sent me to a more racially mixed school.

I give up and go outdoors. Another thunderstorm. Horse-drawn tourist carriages slither by under sheets of rain that look like tinsel in the sunlight. I make the mistake of trying to walk toward the Visitors' Center to pick up my car and am immediately soaked. A car swerves to avoid a puddle, hits another one and sends muddy water rushing over my ankles. "*Fuck* the Chinese," I growl. It is nearly five o'clock and the town is about to close. I give up the idea of walking at last and hitch a ride with one of the tourist buses back to the Visitors' Center. During the ride I sit shivering in the air-conditioning next to an older couple from Alabama chatting about the beautiful crepe myrtle with our bus driver. "So beautiful," the woman chirps under her stiff confection of auburn curls. "So colorful here!"

"Excuse me, what's crepe myrtle?" I ask, rubbing my arms fiercely. The couple stares. The driver turns and grins at me.

"Where you from?" she says brightly.

When I moved to Georgia for Joseph, giving up my teaching job, at first I was euphoric with the change but then, as the months dragged on and on and still no long-term job opportunities could be dug up, irritable. The feeling increased when I had to start relying on him financially as my savings drained away. It manifested itself in a sudden fear of being driven in a car, the irrational belief Joseph would crash on the highway. After a few months it even started to change the way I looked at Georgia and the South, which seemed to grow less penetrable as I spent more and more hours alone in the apartment. It seemed that out there lay a mysterious world in which people were employed, married, active according to social rules I increasingly could not understand. After a while, everything outside the apartment felt threatening to me, something I could not control or anticipate.

To combat this feeling, on weekends Joseph traveled for work, I drove out to the Appalachian Trail or out through the small towns of north Georgia, getting lost on roads winding through acres of trees that looked blue in the distance. An hour's driving blurred all the highways into one long stand of trees and homemade bill-board ads for boiled peanuts and peaches. So far out of Atlanta, my fears dissipated. I didn't want to stop. I could finally enjoy freedom: alone at the wheel, steering my way through uncharted territories.

I think about this freedom driving along the Trace for dinner, away from Natchez. I almost didn't come to Mississippi at all, for fear of—what?—everything, I suppose. Now, thinking about how I will probably find nothing about Opal here, about how uneventful this trip will most likely be, I am actually relieved to have taken the journey. To celebrate, I stop for a meal at a small chain restaurant, six o'clock, pulling a bulky cardigan over my dress. Inside, the waitress ushers me toward the middle of the restaurant a few feet from a table of men dressed in black T-shirts, greasy ball caps, torn jeans and work boots. They are white and of indeterminate age. As I sit down I notice one of the men nudge his nearest companion and begin staring at me. I swallow and shift the menu in my hands. Soon all three of them are staring at me, smoking their cigarettes down to the nub, occasionally making quiet comments to one another. I pointedly stare at my menu, then my book, and never look up. I sneak looks to see whether they have stopped staring when my food comes. They haven't. Their half-finished food begins to congeal on their plates, covered over with a fine gray film of ash.

Half an hour passes; they are still looking. Each of the men has gone either to the bathroom or to the cashier for matches during this time and each has walked by my table, deliberately close and slowly. I clear my throat and keep reading. I eat in tiny swallows.

When they finally leave twenty minutes later, I watch their slim backs closely as they grow smaller in the parking lot, till they get in their pickup and drive. I pay for my meal and hurry out, intent on making it to Natchez before dark.

Is it because I'm a stranger? Because I'm a woman alone? Half Chinese? Every time I turn around here I am confronted with another way I might perceive myself—a kaleidoscope view with a million glittering edges. Which is the most accurate or dangerous one, which the one that matters most here? This is my fascination with Opal in Mississippi. At some level it has nothing to do with Opal. It has to do with Mississippi.

I think about the portrait I have composed of my great-aunt in the 1930s South. A young woman, fresh from China, married to a good-looking man who keeps her in the store all day to serve customers because she speaks English so well. She has children she can't get into the right schools, almost no friends, lives above the rancid meat and powdered-milk smells of a grocery store. Maybe her husband beats her, maybe he doesn't. Maybe her neighbors snub her when she walks outdoors or are friendly. Regardless, she's dependent on her husband and isolated and unhappy. Outside there's what? The Natchez Trace and a small town once filled with millionaires, now dead or gone, their beautiful porches crumbling around them.

I am thinking I need to give this journey up.

At seven all the stores in Natchez have closed; there are only the bars and gambling. I go to my motel, shower, nap, wake up immediately and panic. The knob on my door has turned; there is scratching outside my window. I hold my breath and sneak toward the clunking air conditioner, turn it off to listen. Nothing. Again. Nothing. I peer out the window toward where I can see the forested edge of the Trace beginning, green and enormous, chugging with cicadas. There is something about that strip of green on darker green that keeps me checking the chain and weak double lock on my motel door intermittently. It dies down in the rushing of cars headed south, the highway's insistent traffic. But it flares up the instant I hear a stranger laugh in the parking lot, or the man next door cough while washing. The sound is too close. It feels like it's coming up beside me, filling the space of my empty bed. It's ballooning into the shape of something I should know, and if I watch eventually I'll see it. I stare into the space around me. Something familiar and terrifying.

Ten o'clock. On the *Lady Luck* riverboat I quickly double fifteen dollars in betting chips, lose it all within minutes at the roulette table. The slot machines at each end of the boat clank and whir, spin red lights like little wheels of fire. Cards revolve endlessly with pictures of fruit that never match up. Cherries, apples, a fat pair of lemons.

I think about getting more cash to keep playing out of boredom, but losing wears me out. Just as I am prepared to leave, however, a Chinese couple materializes next to me through the crowd of roulette onlookers and I catch my breath, excited. They are young, and poor-looking. After a few minutes of watching them it becomes apparent that they are not native to the area but tourists like me, and that they both have a tenuous grasp of English. The wife wears a thin blue dress and seems less equipped to deal with the intricacies of American gambling. She hangs back, lets her husband do the talking. He nods and smiles at the young roulette dealer passing out chips.

"You wanna play?" she asks the husband. He fingers the cuffs of his stiff suit jacket. She scowls as he smiles more broadly and waves her hands before the board, indicating that we cannot place any more bets.

"*Play?*" she says again, louder.

He smiles again and the woman turns away wearily.

Then the couple is gone, chattering beside a row of slot machines. I watch the people around the couple watch them. I imagine that there is the same hardening of expression, the same odd stare I've been given all day. Chinese in Mississippi? But I'm the one staring. I turn and walk toward the boat exit, suddenly tired.

Why did Opal ever come to Mississippi? A simple answer: she moved for her husband. Perhaps the better question is really, why did he want her to come to Natchez? According to Po Po, it had been his idea simply to pick up and move south, to one of the smallest and best-preserved pre–Civil War towns. In time, he probably thought, they would blend in, disappear.

After a day and a half of searching, they do seem to have disappeared. If Natchez ever did have Chinese, it seems to have simply swallowed them up in time, absorbed them into its bloodstream the way a very small splinter in a hand can be forgotten, broken down by the body and carried off. I cannot help but think that to go in search of this splinter is to disturb what might be only a trace element in a delicate weave of flesh and muscle. Perhaps it is healthier simply to let the past rest, whatever past there is, however small it may be. "Black, white, Chinese, we're all in here together," the Visitors' Center clerk said. Was that pride in her voice? What did she think I meant by the question? As a northerner, what *did* I mean by this question? Why was it so important that I find Chinese in Natchez, Mississippi?

I remember on a trip I took with my mother to Jamaica, becoming embarrassed by her insistence on photographing all the Chinese restaurants we came across. "Why is this important?" I had whined. Now I am the one photographing Chinese laundry signs, circling Chinese restaurant names on my tourist map. I am the one with the stubborn wish to find importance where there might not be any: some difference greater than the mere *appearance* of difference; a culture I could clearly define. But there are no such borders for me, being Eurasian, though there may be ones for my mother, for her mother, for Opal. I stomp off the boat, drive back to my motel. Like it or not, I am here, too, among the black and white and Chinese. I am one of the people thrown simply into the mix, filling in a family and identity with— when I can't find fact—perhaps its more truthful, emotionally potent, fiction.

The Historic Natchez Foundation is quiet, air-conditioned, friendly. I swish through the doors in baggy shorts, a T-shirt formless enough to feel comfortable in. The secretary gives me an odd smile when I ask my Chinese question but quickly ushers me in to talk with an older, heavyset white woman named Meme. Meme soon tells me that what I want is really the Delta region which has Chinese, not Natchez. She tilts her head. She's in a long skirt, with glasses and short curling white hair. She does have a memory though, come to think of it, a slight memory, of pictures of a Chinese family that once lived here.

"Know any names?" she asks. I do not, which is one of the reasons I haven't bothered to look in the phone book. I have no idea who I would or could call. That's when I realize exactly how stupid this trip is. I have come all the way to Natchez, Mississippi, to find traces of Opal and I do not know her last name from her first marriage.

"Well, there was a grocery," Meme begins, and I start nodding frantically. "And there was a family that lived above the grocery, I think, and I think we have pictures of them somewhere . . ."

She beckons to a young man rifling through some drawers. He says he saw them in the file for the 1876 building. Meme shuffles to a set of brown file cabinets and pulls out a folder from the top drawer. In the file are pictures of a narrow two-storied building with a porch, what may have been the window display of Opal's grocery. Finally, two photographs of a Chinese family. I can almost hear my blood in my ears as she hands me them. They show a very tall, handsome Chinese man wearing sparkling white pants and a white shirt, a black tie and, in one of the photos, a charcoal double-breasted jacket. In the breast pocket of this jacket just peeks a white triangle of a handkerchief, like the beginning of a distress signal.

With him in the pictures are his children: both with bowl cuts, chubby knees and faces, one in a sailor dress that balloons away from her as if she stood over an air vent, a young Marilyn Monroe. The other child sits in a wooden high chair grabbing for the older sister. I am unsure whether this is a boy or girl. They are on the porch of the 1876 building. I examine both pictures closely, hoping to see any evidence of a woman in the window, perhaps watching, but there is none. No Opal. She would be the only person I would know.

"There they are," Meme says. "I think the family sent them to us for records. The building still exists. It's 604 Franklin now, if you want to take a look."

"You don't know the name of the family?" I ask.

"Now we can find it in the phone book," she replies. She disappears into a side room behind a Xerox machine and emerges with several ragged copies of the Natchez phone book for the years between 1912 and 1929.

"I found the name," she says, flipping through one of the books. "Wang. His name was T. E. Wang. He ran the Self-Service Grocery and his wife's name was Opal."

An electric thrill zips through me. "How do you know that?" I ask.

"It's next to his in parentheses. These books list the names, addresses, occupations and spouse names of everyone in town." I go over to see and, indeed, there it is: Opal, in parentheses.

"Do you remember if there were there any other Chinese here?" I ask. Meme pauses and calls out a man's name. A middle-aged man comes out of his office, listens to our questions and adds that there was another Chinese family, a man who ran a laundro-mat on Main Street. He points out another series of old phone books the society has kept in its library for research and shows me where to look. I search to find the dates that Opal lived in Natchez.

"I just remembered," he adds, ducking his head around the stack I am studying in, "that the Wangs' children were home-schooled. They couldn't go to the white schools. In fact that might be why they moved. I'm pretty sure there's no family remaining from them," he says, scratching his head. "We would have known about that."

After a few minutes with the phone books I discover that T. E. Wang, along with Opal, moved to Natchez around 1928, set up the Self-Service and stayed until 1940. Around 1941, the Wangs are gone and Wah You and Yep Saw Wang own the business. They run it until 1946, after which date there is no mention of Wangs in the phone book again. Wah You himself arrived in Natchez around 1935 to help out with the business, most likely a brother or close relation. When Opal divorced T.E. and left is unclear. Phone books are missing; dates of arrival and departure cannot be located in these records.

I rifle through the phone books, looking through other years. I even check for other names: Chinns, Mars, Tsaos, Tiens. For the period from 1897 to 1946 there are only two Chinese families in Natchez and they did not even live here concurrently. Opal's family, I am beginning to understand, *was* the Chinese community in Natchez.

"You can use the Xerox machine over there to make copies of the photos," Meme tells me, interrupting my calculations.

I do and that is when I see, flipping over the photo of the handsome man in his charcoal jacket, the address: Mrs. Marianne Wang, ———— Street, Seattle. It is Opal's eldest daughter's name. It is Aunt Opal's address.

I have to work to conceal my excitement at discovering I am indeed looking at Opal's first husband and children. I am looking at evidence of her life. I do not explain any of this to Meme, however. I have already told her that I was a university student doing a sociology paper. "Wonderful," Meme had said. "I never thought about the Chinese in Natchez before."

Meme sees my expression and walks over.

"Address," I manage to get out. "I found an address." Again Meme looks delighted.

For some reason, however, I do not feel comfortable. I am torn between wanting to reveal my purpose here and to continue to hide it. My omission is irrational, I know; why—how—should I be afraid of Meme? But I am afraid. I am afraid of identifying myself and my purpose, and blame it on the fact that I am in the South. That's when I realize that this has nothing to do with the South.

"I'm sorry we don't have more for you to go on," Meme says.

"This is fine, it's really more than enough," I reply, thanking her. "I didn't expect to find anything."

"Well, you can always contact the family in Seattle. Perhaps she's still alive."

"Maybe," I say carefully. "But I doubt it. It's been a while."

When I think about my Aunt Opal I regret saying what I did about marriage and children. She was a deeply religious, tender woman and socially conservative. What did I know about love and sacrifice at age twelve? But if Opal and I ever were similar, it was in our ways of saying what might be surprising, even shocking, to those around us. This is what I miss about her. Opal's great difference from her family was that she would talk about the ugly things in life, the strangeness, the race. Driving around the hot streets of Natchez, I wonder whether it was the isolation of being the only Chinese during what must have been a hard time in Mississippi that made Opal this way. Meanwhile, immersed in a West Coast Chinatown, Po Po could afford to be silent, not thinking or caring to think how she was different from those around her. Opal would not have seen anything but differences, the blacks sitting in clusters on beer crates in her store, the whites passing indifferently on the street. I travel past block after empty block of preserved—if badly—history, in antique shops and antebellum mansions, and feel cast adrift on an island of the past, where I might just be the only Chinese in Natchez.

I have to admit I am ashamed for wanting to understand what this means. As ashamed as Po Po is of talking about her history, as ashamed as she must have been of seeing her children isolated in America by their appearance, their cultural differences. And yet, when I think of those hard, irritated stares I get sometimes from white strangers who discover my racial background in conversation or by accident, when I recall a man telling me angrily I shouldn't talk about it because it isn't important, I rebel. I become like Opal: I start to talk and talk about all the embarrassing things. This is the past, yes. But it is the present, too, and the future; wishing race out of existence is not the same as its simply not existing.

And now I realize what a perfect place I have come to for resuscitating the past, this shame of race and meaning, violence, history. Everywhere are signs of it. Horse carriages, posters for old-time dances, the occasional Confederate bumper sticker and gun rack. What would it be like to live in an area that represents the glory of the Confederate past seen suddenly through the eyes of a northerner? And a northerner looking for, of all things, Chinese? How can the past help but sound grotesque, fabulous? This is what Po Po knows, sitting by herself at home, refusing to talk about her life. This is what the woman at the Visitors' Center hopes, giving help to people like me while insisting I am just like her. I cannot exoticize her town into an anecdote. These are people's lives. No one wants to be victim to someone else's storytelling.

Perhaps this is why I did not approach the lawyer in the window. I have no idea whether he would have identified himself as Chinese, whether he would have thought of his ethnic heritage as important enough to discuss with a stranger. I also have no idea whether my identifying him as someone *I* see as Chinese would have offended him; possibly he never thought of himself or the Chinese as separate from white Natchez. As I think about him, I keep returning to that phrase—"we're all in here together"—its casual dismissal of difference, place, reality. Is this what Opal, living in Natchez with her first husband, tried to learn? That nothing distinguished herself from her neighbors except what she wanted to distinguish herself? Traveling around Asia and the States, I am certainly no different in this. Perhaps I am afraid to become as my appearance suggests—"merely white"—because then I have nothing to distinguish me. Or maybe it is because, entering completely that vast world of whiteness I have always seen as partly outside myself, I'm afraid that I will lose control, disappear.

And, frankly, I must disappear if race is to be simply white and other, not fluidly interchangeable. We are "all in here together," if "here" is the predicament of defining identity. But once "here" becomes as specific as a place on a map, an ethnicity, the truth of the phrase breaks down. Race was not a choice for Opal in Mississippi. It was not a place we could enter or leave at will. And, searching for traces of Opal here, I find that race is not really a choice for me, either, like traveling to one town and not to another. I am not one of the ones "all in here together." For me to choose to become one ethnicity so that I can define myself for strangers is to fall victim to a monolithic, constructed idea of race that nothing in my personal history would support as true. At some point Opal and I are very different and no discovery of her past will change this fact. But ethnicity, for me, is not Chinese America versus white America. Unlike Opal, I cannot choose one identity without losing half of myself.

My last afternoon in Natchez I spend driving around the Trace, looking at the ruined buildings, the historic battle sites. Searching for a short hiking trail I might take, I turn off onto one of the side roads and drive past fields and farmhouses, the sun drifting high above the trees. I speed up, get lost, find the main highway again. This is the search for more adventure. As the small road curves I see what looks like a long piece of dark rope lying across both lanes. I thoughtlessly speed toward it, smack over its bulk just as I realize what I am driving on is a snake. "Oh!" I cry and stop the car, backing up and accidentally hitting it again. I have never seen a snake outside a terrarium. I step out of the car to take a closer look.

The snake's slab head oozes out a thick broth of red and green and gray. Its scales are soft brown and white, ruffled-looking. It is huge: longer than the length of my arm and nearly as wide around as my bicep. I am both delighted and frightened seeing it here, on this road, under my car. One of us seems to be misplaced. Shouldn't something so wild be where I can't see it, lurking in tall grasses, not traveling along on a stretch of still-warm concrete? Flies dip and flicker along its head. The sun is starting to set now; I need to leave. I get back into the car and feel my hands shake with what feels like exultation. But then my camera slips from the passenger seat to the floor, I bend down to recover it, deciding immediately to take a picture of my accidental kill. The thought of forgetting it makes the thing suddenly precious. I need the image preserved in black and white. I need to take the memory of it back home.

Acknowledgments

Thanks to the Hopwood Foundation for their award for "We Do Not Live Here, We Are Only Visitors"; to the Lions' Clubs of Seattle and Kobe, Japan; to Fulbright and the Korean-American Educational Commission; to John Fulton, Nancy Strauss and Lee Behlman for reading the essays (even if they didn't appear between these covers); to Leigh Feldman and the Darhansoff & Verrill Literary Agency for all their critical brilliance; to Robin Desser for her insight; to my parents; to Mrs. Patricia Kan and Mrs. Irene Stubbs for patience; to Arnicia Fleming, Amalie Weber, Gene Tien, Melissa McCulloch, Charles Forster, and Greg Beckelhymer; to Shumai (I'll take you on that walk now); to Lee Won Hee, Kang Min Sok, and the staff of Usok Girls' High School; to Eric Heiman—always Eric Heiman; and finally to my piano teacher, Catherine Lampman, for teaching me timing, music, discipline.

About the Author

Paisley Rekdal attended the University of Washington and Trinity College Dublin as an undergraduate and received an M.A. in Medieval Studies from the University of Toronto and an M.F.A. from the University of Michigan. She is the recipient of a Hopwood and a Fulbright award, and she has published poems and essays in *Poetry Northwest*, the *Sonora Review*, *Crab Orchard Review*, and the *Chattahoochee Review*, among other publications and anthologies. Her book of poems, *A Crash of Rhinos*, will be published by the University of Georgia Press in Fall 2000. She was born and raised in Seattle, Washington, and now lives in Wyoming.

DATE DUE

OCT 2 2013	

DEMCO, INC. 38-2931